Other books by Patricia Taylor Wells

The Eyes of the Doe
Mademoiselle Renoir à Paris
Lodestar
The Sand Rose
Kaleidoscope
Carousel
Maple Point

FOR the LOVE of Eskies

For the Love
of Eskies

Patricia Taylor Wells

Bink Books
Bedazzled Ink Publishing Company • Fairfield, California

978-1-960373-80-9 paperback

Cover Design
by

Sapling
Studio

Bink Books
a division of
Bedazzled Ink Publishing Company
Fairfield, California
http://www.bedazzledink.com

Kaspar
(graphite on Bristol board, C.A. Casey)

KEIKO'S STORY

June 25, 1985 — February 5, 2002

OUR DOG KEIKO came to us on a bright, beautiful Saturday morning—a little furball who changed our lives forever. We got her for all the wrong reasons, yet nothing in our lives has ever been so right. We had begun thinking about getting a dog after realizing that the children we had hoped for were not in the stars for us. We researched numerous dog breeds but kept returning to the American Eskimo Dog with its exceptional beauty. It was no surprise that Eskies, as they are commonly called, were referred to as the "Dog Beautiful." But even though we knew the breed of dog we wanted, we weren't sure the timing was right or if we were ready and willing to take on the responsibility of caring for one.

That decision was made for us suddenly and alarmingly at one ordinary end of the day in August. Evening's quietness was beginning to settle as Bob and I chatted, mainly about the littleness of our day. It was seven o'clock, but we were in no hurry to prepare dinner. Now that I no longer worked outside of our home, my schedule was guided more by my whims than the clock.

I heard a thump, followed by another. Maybe a tree limb had fallen, or a careless bird had struck a window. A third knock, louder this time, seemed to come from the front door. Bob got up and headed that way. I heard the door open, followed by two or three unfamiliar guttural voices and words I could not understand. I immediately ran toward the foyer, where Bob lay on the bottom steps of the stairway with a gun pressed against his forehead. Three young men, all wielding pistols, had pushed their way into our home. I stood there, trying to make sense of what was going on.

Were they there to rob us, I wondered. I assumed that the intruders were Vietnamese or a close ethnic group, and perhaps even gang members. They couldn't have been more than twenty years old. Their squinted eyes were as dark as night, and their thick black hair stood in little spikes. Their skin was the color of a Kraft envelope. Although their frames were slight and their stature short, the weapons they flaunted made them powerful, menacing, and unpredictable.

As Bob pleaded for the men to leave, I heard his assailant's gun cock. I queezed my eyes and stopped breathing, but nothing happened. One of the men moved closer to me, aiming the barrel of his handgun at my chest. The third man paced back and forth, nervously looking out the front room windows. I surmised that he was their lookout.

I stood with my feet cemented to the floor as my mind swirled in a strange universe that was half dream and half real. I blacked out momentarily, fearing the worst. When I opened my eyes, my heart pounded like a racehorse at full gallop as my instincts kicked in, and I started running for my life. As I reached the back door, the man who had targeted me with his gun caught up with me. He grabbed my arm just as I clutched the doorknob. I could almost feel his breath against my skin as he uttered harsh, foreign words, He pulled me back into the family room, but I was able to break away from him. Once more, I ran to the back door, screaming for help once the door opened wide. Everything felt like a slow-motion haze, and my long, high-pitched cry sounded like a whisper.

I had not even gotten outside before the man clutched the necklace I was wearing. I felt the gold chain dig into my neck as it separated and fell to the floor. My pursuer dragged me back into the family room, shouting for me to get down as he pointed his weapon at the floor. There was no time to think, no time to utter a prayer. The only power I had was my refusal to get down. I don't know where that strength came from, but it made me feel responsible for my fate.

I stood across from the man, searching his eyes for whatever mercy they had. Without warning, he turned away from me and rushed toward the foyer. I heard the door slam and looked out the front window as the three men and the getaway driver sped down the street.

I heard Bob moan and then shout, "Jesus Christ!" It was a sound of relief since I had not known if he was dead or alive. Bob locked the door and told me to call the sheriff. I was so rattled that I couldn't even provide our address or a description of the gang members.

We had no idea why we had been targeted for a home invasion. There seemed to be no sense in it. Why us, we wondered. It was still daylight outside. We lived in a middle-class neighborhood where crime was rarely seen. The sheriff took notes, but there was little else he could do other than contact the Houston police to see if they knew anything, perhaps about a similar case.

We were terrified and quickly decided we could not sleep in our home that evening. One of our neighbors offered to let us stay with them. We barely slept, and as soon as we ate breakfast the following day, we began doing whatever we could to feel safe in our home. We hired a company to install bars on our windows and doors, even though doing so was against homeowners' regulations. But that wasn't enough to make us feel safe. Getting a dog for protection made more sense than getting a gun.

A few days later, the Houston police asked Bob and me to come downtown for questioning. Bob and I were interviewed separately about the home invasion. Unknown to us, they had rounded up a Vietnamese Mafia gang matching the description we had given authorities after the break-in. Neither of us could say that any of the five men in the lineup was ever in our home. After a while, we learned that one of the former Generals of the South Vietnamese Army had lived with his family two doors away from us. The FBI had held him under surveillance, but either they didn't know or weren't saying that he had died of natural causes a few weeks before our incident. Many years later, Bob and I resolved the mystery to our satisfaction. When we moved to our neighborhood, we purchased the house that had been used as the sales office. We believe the General had been using the office address in connection with financial loans he may have had with the mafia gang. Since he had passed away, the loan was likely in arrears, which may explain why the break-in had occurred.

I knew nothing about adopting a dog. I almost gave up finding one before spotting an ad in the Houston paper. "American Eskimo Pups," it read. Even though the breeder

"Dogs have a way of finding the people who need them and filling an emptiness they didn't even know they had."
— Thom Jones, Author

was from out of town, I dialed the number anyway. We wanted a lovable dog who wouldn't hesitate to take a chunk out of anyone who threatened us. My voice shook as I explained to the breeder how our lives had been turned upside down after three members of a gang had burst into our home and held us at gunpoint. I worried that maybe I had shared too much information about why we wanted a dog that was liable to bite, even if not provoked.

Breeders, however, know that while Eskies are very devoted to their families, they are also wary of strangers. The breed was not well-known in the United States until the 1960s. Before then, they had primarily lived in backyards and on farms, surprisingly unnoticed, considering their beauty.

We agreed to meet the breeder in a parking lot near our home the following Saturday morning. We spotted a young woman standing beside a van as

"It's not the size of the dog in the fight; it's the size of the fight in the dog."
— Mark Twain

we pulled up. At her feet was a teeny white furball pacing back and forth. We were in love at first sight. The breeder had lost the pedigree for the pup's father, which meant she could not be offered as a purebred. We didn't care about that. What we saw was all we needed to know. Considering how haphazardly we acquired her, it was remarkable that she turned out to be such a perfect match for us.

When I set our little bundle down on the floor in her new home, she trembled as she walked up against the baseboards. We kept our distance until she felt safe enough to lie down. Seeing her crouched next to the wall with her ears folded back and tail tucked between her legs almost broke my heart. She was frightened of us. She had been snatched away from her mother and littermates, handed over to strangers, and thrust into a strange new world without her consent. I had imagined a much better homecoming.

We named our little girl Keiko, which means "blessed child" or "adored" in Japanese. It suited her. She had a splendid white coat that sparkled in the sun. Her dark nose and mouth accentuated her delicate muzzle. Her eyelashes were as white as snow, a trait often overlooked due to the dark rims around her eyes. We usually called her "Little Girl" later on because that's what she was to us. We centered our world on her, ensuring her needs were always met, even before ours.

Bob and I had only been married two years when Keiko came into our lives. A few months before, I had put my career on hold, hoping that a less stressful life improved our chances of having children. Although that never happened, we chose not to dwell on it. We even considered participating in the Children's Program of Northern Ireland, which pairs a Protestant child with a Catholic child, allowing them to spend the summer together in the United States. The program helped them focus on their similarities and kept many children safe, especially during the violent conflict known as The Troubles. There were benefits to not having children. We had the freedom to come and go as we pleased. We didn't have to take care of or provide for anyone other than ourselves, and we didn't have to establish a college fund or pay for a big wedding one day. I found it easy to live with the idea of not having to raise a family, but not having grown children who will come back home for visits in our golden years is an emptiness that can never be fulfilled. Having a dog, though, is satisfactory compensation.

It didn't take much for Keiko to become the "blessed child" we never had. It happened the very first night she was with us. I had made a bed for her in our bathroom. As soon as the lights were out, she began to whimper. I immediately brought her to our bed, where she slept for many years. Few things in life feel as good as a warm puppy nuzzled against your back.

I had never lived with a dog before. When I was growing up, all of our dogs stayed outside. We never got to know them the way you come to know an inside dog. The hazards and temptations of an outside dog's world usually meant they wouldn't be around that long. Our Collie Lady died from fox poisoning that a neighbor had put out in his pasture. When backing out of our driveway after visiting us, my grandfather ran over our Collie puppy, Prince. Our Labrador Retriever, Jenju, was shot in the leg by a hunter. He did survive, but later had to be put down after both his legs gave out. We hardly said a prayer before digging a hole and burying their mangled bodies. Grieving over a dog was not something we did, even alone. A dog was just a dog. Or so I thought back then. The greatest joy in life comes from our ability to love another being. It doesn't matter whether that being is human or not.

> *"Life has a way of presenting us with everything we need exactly when we need it."*
> — *Patricia Taylor Wells*

People often wonder how the American Eskimo Dog got its name, a breed most likely never used as a sled dog. The dog's appearance may have contributed to it. Eskies have a voluminous ruff around the chest and shoulders and a tail that curls over their backs, similar to those of the Siberian Huskies, Alaskan Malamutes, and Samoyeds found in Alaska and across the Arctic. The real story, however, had more to do with the German immigrants who settled in America's Midwest in the early 1800s. Their German Spitz dogs accompanied them, serving as all-around farmhands. Immigrants, especially those from Germany, preferred living in areas like Wisconsin, Minnesota, and Ohio, which reminded them of the German countryside.

The German word "spitz," meaning "sharp point," describes how quickly the breed's ears rise to a sharp point when alerted. During World War I, anti-German sentiment grew rapidly, which resulted in the German Spitz's name being changed to American Spitz in 1924. The dog's name was changed again to American Eskimo Spitz a year later as a tribute to an American couple who bred Spitz dogs and ran a kennel known as American Eskimo Kennels. In 1926, the dog's name was shortened to American Eskimo. The breed was recognized by the American Kennel Club in 1994.

Eskies come in three sizes: toy, miniature, and standard. Keiko was a standard, which usually weighed no more than thirty-five pounds. Their fur is either entirely white or white with touches of biscuit cream, and is kept clean by the natural oils on their fur that prevent dirt from sticking to their coat. Their magnificent plumed tail is carried over their back as they parade for all to admire. Another feature is that Eskies always smile, especially when they look deeply into their owner's eyes.

Raising a puppy had its challenges. We had to consider another life that depended on us for its existence. House training and establishing rules of behavior are not easy tasks. We were novices at both. We sometimes wondered if we had enough patience and love to survive Keiko's upbringing. Anyone who has raised a puppy has a long list of terrible things it has managed to do. Keiko was no exception. She enjoyed being mischievous. Keiko chewed the leg of a small table down to the size of a toothpick. She tore off the skirts of two sofas. She ate a hole in a vinyl floor. She stole the napkins off our laps at dinner time. She ripped off the covers of magazines and shredded them into bits. She tore open any stuffed animal we gave her and pulled out its cotton filling. She grabbed my ankles with her front paws each time the telephone rang, hoping she could prevent me from answering it. No matter what she did, we loved her. It took a lot of patience to cure her of all of her mischief, the same patience it takes to nurture, understand, help, heal, and, most of all, love another being.

After Keiko had been with us a few weeks, she decided to test the rank and hierarchy of her newly established dog pack, two-thirds of which were

"Patience is not just a virtue; it is the best remedy for every trouble."
— Titus Maccius Plautus,
254–184 B.C.

human. I became her adversary. She sat on the fireplace hearth or the bottom shelf of an end table, waiting for me to enter the room. As soon as I was in the center of the room, totally vulnerable in its open space, she flew off the hearth or shelf and ran circles around me. Her sharp little teeth bit my ankles and then my hands as I waved them to ward her off. I screamed in terror and jumped on the sofa to escape her, giving her good reason to believe she was the top dog among us. Something had to be done. The advice in a book by dog expert Barbara Woodhouse caught my attention. As suggested in the book, I donned Bob's raincoat, a pair of boots, and thick leather gloves. Keiko and I then went out back for a good old-fashioned dog fight. I let her come at me from all angles without flinching an inch. Her razor-sharp teeth were useless against my protective gear. She soon gave up. I had overcome my problem by facing it.

Like most well-meaning parents do with their children, we unintentionally transferred some of our negative traits to Keiko. Within

"Fear always makes the wolf bigger than he is."
— German proverb

a very short time, she had picked up on how anxious we became every time the doorbell rang. We were afraid to open the door. We worried that someone on the other side would force their way in again and hold us at gunpoint. We had turned our home into a prison by installing bars on our windows and securing our doors with extra locks, even though an electronic alarm system monitored them. By Halloween, our apprehension had grown out of control. Even though we knew it was only trick-or-treaters ringing the doorbell that evening, we were afraid to answer it. Finally, we grabbed Keiko and got into the car.

We drove around the neighborhood until we were sure all the children had gone home. Nothing we had done to protect ourselves had made us feel any better. Like us, Keiko was fearful when the doorbell rang, but not once had she ever jumped when a thunderclap burst in the air. I didn't have to wonder why; I knew the answer. Bob and I always remained calm during a storm, and that was what we communicated to Keiko. The only way we could ever feel safe again was to change our thinking. We had to stop expecting someone to attack us. We decided that a change of scenery was what we needed. However, you cannot run away from a problem. It will follow you wherever you go. Sometimes, though, a fresh start can put you on the right path. Bob began looking for a job in Virginia. Neither of us had ever been there, but it appealed to us. Eventually, he was offered a job in Richmond. The real estate market in Houston was down, and it looked like it would take a long time before we had a buyer. I didn't want to stay in Houston alone, so I packed everything and stored it.

"Inner peace does not come from actual conditions but from what we choose to believe about those conditions."
— *Patricia Taylor Wells*

One night, about a week before our move, I noticed that Keiko had scratched a small opening in a carpet seam. The hole was in the center of the room, where a piece of furniture could not hide it. I was sure I could repair it by cutting another piece of carpet to fit the opening to plug the hole. Not satisfied with my first attempt, I cut a new piece of carpet and widened the original hole to make it fit. This process continued until I found myself staring at a twelve-inch hole. The following day, I made a frantic call to a carpet company and arranged for someone to come and fix the mess I had made. As soon as the repairs were finished and the workers were gone, I began vacuuming up all the scraps they had left behind in case anyone came to look at the house. Keiko was still wearing the leash I had used to keep her out of the way. Before I knew it, I had sucked the end of the leash into the vacuum. Terrified, Keiko ran in the opposite direction while I chased her with the vacuum, screaming for her to stop. Her little neck was being choked as I struggled to keep up with her in our wild chase around the room. I was so focused on making Keiko stop running that I failed to realize I had complete control over what was happening. All I had to do was turn off the vacuum.

One advantage of moving to Virginia was that we could drive to the Finger Lakes in upstate New York, where Bob's parents had a cottage on Keuka Lake. Bob had gone there almost every summer since he was six months old. We had also spent a week of our honeymoon at their historic home, Maple Point. We were especially pleased that we could now take Keiko with us. We had never boarded her, primarily because of the neighbors who kept her when we traveled.

"Sometimes, we make things more complicated than necessary by trying to control everyone's actions but our own."
— *Patricia Taylor Wells*

It didn't take long for me to become enthralled by how beautiful, peaceful, and relaxing Maple Point could be. Over the years, we enjoyed many hours on the front porch overlooking the lake. It was a place where worries died and dreams were born. Our memories of Keiko swimming in the pristine waters of Keuka Lake, watching a full moon rise above the hills as we sat with her on the steps of the dock house, and zipping across the lake in the motor boat with the wind and spray slapping our faces are the kinds of memories that will live forever and the kinds of moments that make life grand.

Going to the cottage every year was the only constant thing in our lives. It was a haven from a noisy world and a refuge in a world of change. Following our marriage, we lived in six cities during the twenty-two years we spent at Maple Point. It was sometimes difficult to leave old friends behind, but the ones who mattered would always be there, regardless of where we went.

Virginia was one of our favorite places. Early on, we became good friends with three other couples who had moved there from

Houston. Brad and Mike had also worked at the same bank as Bob in Houston. The third couple lived two houses down from us. We took turns having everyone over for dinner, followed by a game of cards. After I accepted a job as an office assistant at a real estate agency, my neighbor down the street took care of Keiko's needs until I was home. Her children adored Keiko and chased her in our backyard. The children often came over and asked if they could play with her, especially if it had snowed. We bundled Keiko in a dog jacket, and the kids chased her until they wore her out. Poor Keiko sometimes ran and hid as soon as she saw them.

During this time, we slowly overcame the ordeal we had experienced in Houston. Our house was small but charming. Hosting events and visitors was challenging, but we always made the best of things. Our Houston neighbors, Paul and JoAnn, spent several days with us. We enjoyed showing them all the historic places in our area. Both our parents were also guests, whom we enjoyed entertaining.

My parents surprised us by driving from Texas to Virginia to see us. They rarely went anywhere other than to see family members in East Texas, so we usually had to visit them if we wanted to see them. Texas also had its moments, though. I have always loved taking Keiko's picture in the middle of a bluebonnet field. She was lovely in her brilliant white coat, surrounded by deep blue flowers.

Our most memorable visit was with our friends Glenda and Jerry and their three daughters. They had moved to New Orleans in 1986, so I had invited them to spend Thanksgiving with us. We had not seen them since they moved from Houston to Bakersfield, California, soon after Bob and I were married. I also invited my former Houston neighbors to join us. Their son and my friend's oldest daughter, Stephanie, were the same age. Ironically, both couples had twins of the same age: two girls, Kerry and Michelle, and the neighbors' set, a boy and a girl. Having children as our guests made our holiday get-together more festive.

However, the children were soon grumbling. My biggest mistake was setting a children's table with decorative turkey place cards. No one liked their assigned seating. By the end of dinner,

I had a migraine, and perhaps Keiko did, too. She stayed out of the way as much as possible. But eventually, all was well. Many years later, when we attended the wedding of Glenda and Jerry's daughter Kerry, all three girls remembered Keiko but not us. We had communicated by mail over the twenty-plus years since we had seen each other. We now see them two or three times a year.

Later on, I interviewed for a job with the newly formed Virginia Lottery. It was a fascinating job, very fast-paced and demanding. I made sure before accepting that I had time to run home at lunch each day and take care of Keiko. I always put her above everything else in my life.

Bob always enjoyed driving down Monument Avenue to and from work. In 2020, a controversy over the monuments resulted in their eventual removal. For many, the once-renowned sculptures were considered offensive, built to intimidate African Americans and to promote white supremacy. Fortunately, the monuments sculpted by Bob's great-great-uncle, Henry Kirke Bush-Brown, were not removed or targeted. Of course, his great-great-uncle was on the opposing side of the fence, and his three equestrian bronze sculptures can still be seen at the Gettysburg Battlefield.

Another thing we enjoyed in Richmond was the flickering candles in each window during the Christmas holidays. It was a simple display, cozy and festive, dating back to colonial times when lit candles were viewed as a welcoming sign. However, watching Keiko unwrap her Christmas gifts made everything bright and beautiful.

Keiko loved to run in our fenced backyard. It was large enough for her to wear herself out. We had also inherited a garden that the former owners had planted. It was severely neglected due to my lack of gardening knowledge and unwillingness to devote the required time. Soon, there were dried-up watermelon vines and overgrown cucumbers no one wanted. Keiko occasionally inspected the few vegetables and fruits struggling to survive. Eventually, we planted rose bushes and other flowering plants in the neglected space. I was satisfied that I didn't have to do much of anything from then on.

Keiko never liked going on walks that much. And if we stopped to talk with someone, she grew impatient. She liked riding in the car on Saturday mornings when Bob went to the cleaners, but she barked whenever the vehicle stopped at a traffic light or the ride came to an end. We never knew why.

Things began to unravel after we had lived in Richmond for about four years. One of the former Houston couples we hung out with was divorced. While that was unfortunate, none of us were prepared for the tragedy that befell the other former Houston couple whose son and his former girlfriend were murdered. Perhaps what happened could have been prevented, but it is impossible to know for sure. The incident made me pause and wonder how we had escaped such a similar outcome, and they hadn't. It was very sad, and nothing was ever the same.

We were disappointed that a bank in Georgia was acquiring the bank where Bob worked. Bob was transferred to Atlanta. The only advantage I could see was that my parents, who still lived in Texas, would be closer to us. We missed Richmond. It was a city rich in history and tradition. Despite how things had ended for our friends there, I preferred living in Virginia rather than Georgia.

Although we had enjoyed living in Richmond, we never returned there. We often took road trips through Virginia, but never detoured in that direction for whatever reason. At the time, it was my dream town. Perhaps I didn't want to return because I knew it would never be the same, even if I did.

"Life is a journey, not a destination."
— *Ralph Waldo Emerson*

Keiko was six when we moved to Atlanta. Not long after our move, she developed a large hematoma on one of her ear flaps that required surgical removal. Several times a day before her surgery, Bob and I gently massaged her ear and quietly affirmed that it would heal. She was a pitiful sight. The night before her operation, the ear was just as swollen as it had been. Still, we continued to imagine her ear surrounded by a white, healing light. The following day, the hematoma had vanished entirely. We couldn't believe it. We took her to the clinic anyway. The veterinarian was just as amazed as we were and sent us home. It typically takes several months for a hematoma to heal on its own, often leaving unsightly scarring behind. We had witnessed spontaneous healing, yet it was no more magnificent or miraculous than the new leaf appearing each spring on a seemingly dead branch. What a wonderful world we live in!

Another benefit we discovered was the Atlanta Unity Church. To our surprise, one of the ministers we had known at the Unity Church in Houston was now serving as the head minister in Atlanta. We quickly got involved in various ways. I was working on a church cookbook and met two new friends, Janis and Nancy. When I discovered that Janis had an Eskie, I asked her if she could recommend a kennel. Now that we were in Atlanta, driving to the Finger Lakes to visit Bob's parents every summer would be difficult, and we did not want Keiko to travel in the belly of an airplane. Without hesitation, Janis said we didn't need a kennel; she would keep Keiko for us. Our little girl had not spent much time with other dogs, so we thought this arrangement would help her become more socialized. One year, we invited our friends, Janis and Nancy, along with their husbands, to spend a week with us at Maple Point. It was the hottest summer I had ever experienced at the Finger Lakes. We were miserable but thankful that Keiko was not there with us. She was in an air-conditioned house of a dog sitter Janis had recommended.

Not long after we had moved to Atlanta, the newly formed C&S/Sovran Bank merged with NationsBank. Bob now had to fly to Dallas headquarters almost every week. His job was very demanding, mainly due to his new boss. Since I worked full-time, I had hired someone to come in daily to let Keiko out.

Neither Keiko nor I liked not having Bob at home most of the time. I was also unhappy with my job, so Bob and I decided we needed a change. It was a difficult decision, as we had enjoyed the friends we had made in Atlanta. We had everything we wanted socially, but the stress of our careers weighed us down. Bob began a job search and quickly interviewed with a bank in Columbus, Ohio. Bob was the only candidate nationwide who met the bank's requirements. During the interview, Bob discovered that the bank's headhunter, whose last name was Wells, was a distant relative. As it turned out, they shared a great-great-grandfather who had traveled on the Oregon Trail.

When Bob contacted George, his former boss in Houston, for a reference, he was surprised when George refused his request. Instead, George, now working for a Pennsylvania bank, wanted to hire Bob for a new position. Since George had always been Bob's favorite boss, he quickly accepted the offer. The bank was situated in Reading, which was unfamiliar to us.

Bob began his new job immediately. Keiko and I were stuck in Atlanta, waiting for our house to sell. We grew impatient, and eventually, we had our belongings put in storage and joined Bob in Reading. Once our Atlanta house was sold, we purchased an older stone house typical of Pennsylvania. We became good friends with two neighbors and are still in touch with them.

Although Keiko had seen snow for the first time when we lived in Virginia, she had never seen as much of it as the blizzard we experienced in Reading. Neither had I. However, Bob grew up in places like Upstate New York, Illinois, and Wisconsin, and knew how to deal with the cold and icy conditions. Our biggest concern was the large ice blocks that formed in the gutters and often fell to the ground unexpectedly. We had to stay on guard when taking Keiko outside. Large sheets of snow and ice would also form on our slate roof and rapidly swoosh down without much warning.

There were many things to like about Reading. We weren't that far away from Amish country, which we found interesting and a reminder that a simple life often outweighs a complicated one. We met some fascinating people after joining the Reading Newcomers Club. Many of them had lived in or traveled to places around the world.

Bob was happy that his commute to work was only four miles from our house to the bank, and working for his former boss was an asset.

We couldn't wait to take Keiko to Maple Point the following summer. The drive from Reading to Keuka Lake was about six hours.

Keiko always joined me in the hammock on the front porch overlooking the lake. It was a favorite pastime. She lay on my lap as I swung us to and fro. Sometimes, my in-laws' dog Maggie tried to jump in with us, but Keiko growled at her until she left us alone. I loved watching the sailboats glide past us, especially when the sky was a brilliant blue. I couldn't imagine a more peaceful setting.

Keiko also enjoyed our boat rides on Keuka Lake's pristine waters. Just being there was like being in heaven.

During this time, I envisioned that one day, Bob and I would spend every summer at Maple Point. Family and friends, though, not the cottage, made this place special. The best times of all were when they were around.

I couldn't have asked for a better life during the next few years. Life was good, yet there was always a shadow hanging over us, and that was change. Nothing ever stays the same. We grow old; we lose friends and family. It's that way with everyone. Our memories are the only things we can hold on to, and even those fade with time. At least most of the time, I could see change as an opportunity rather than a setback.

We had only been in Reading for about two years when I persuaded my parents to fly to Pennsylvania to see us. Bob still had enough airline miles left from his travels to purchase first-class tickets for them. My mother had never flown before and was reluctant to accept our offer. Eventually, she gave in. My parents landed safely and enjoyed their time in Reading.

The weekend before they returned to Texas, Bob was directed to attend a secret meeting on Sunday regarding a potential bank merger between Meridian and CoreStates. Initially, Bob stayed in Reading until the bank conversion was completed. We were disappointed that the merger was taking place and worried that Bob would not have a job in a few months. Fortunately, Bob was transferred to Philadelphia to run the conversion.

Of course, this meant we had to move again. We decided to build a house in West Chester, thirty-five miles outside Philadelphia. Bob could commute to work by train most of the time. The neighborhood we chose was one mile from downtown. There were thirty-two lots, and we were the fourth home built. Getting to know our neighbors little by little was helpful. Keiko seemed to adjust quickly as well.

> *"Sometimes, you gotta create what you want to be part of."*
> — *Geri Weitzman*

In 1997, a year after we had moved into our new home, there were enough neighbors to form a community. I decided the best way to achieve this was to create a newsletter open to everyone who lived in our development, Crosspointe. Once new neighbors moved in, there were dinner parties, holiday get-togethers, spring and fall festivals, children's events, and more. Dogs and cats were also a part of our community. I knew every child and their pet's name. Aside from Maple Point, Crosspointe was the best place on earth.

However, no matter how great a place is, unexpected problems can still arise. Our next-door neighbor decided to build a swimming pool. Her lot was about four to five feet higher than ours. Once the pool was built, she drained it through a hose dropped off the side of our property. She refused to run the hose down her sloped driveway to allow water to flow into the storm drains. My solution was to design and build a fence high enough to block the pool's view and reduce the noise level. It was beautiful, with a pergola gate and New Dawn climbing roses blooming over it. There was also a bench in the backyard with a back panel adorned with wisteria vines rambling above its arbor.

That same year, my great-nephew Ricky from Texas flew to visit us for over a week. We showed him around Philadelphia, Lancaster, and then Washington, D.C. We also had a cookout with our former neighbors in Reading and the neighbors across the street from us in West Chester. Keiko enjoyed having company as much as we did.

The following year, Ricky returned to Pennsylvania for six weeks. This time, we took him to New York City, Hershey, and Keuka Lake for a week with Bob's family at Maple Point. While we enjoyed Ricky's visit, handling a thirteen-year-old who may not have appreciated all we had done for him was sometimes challenging.

Earlier in 1998, a merger with First Union Bank occurred. Bob continued to work for CoreStates for several months, but eventually, his position was eliminated. As he had always done, he immediately began searching for a new job, hopefully in the West Chester area. Neither of us wanted to move again. The Chairman of CoreStates sent the resumes of senior employees being let go to major companies in Philadelphia. Bob received a call from KPMG, one of the Big Four accounting firms. He was reluctant to interview with them since the position was primarily a sales job.

Despite losing his job, I continued to plan Bob's fiftieth birthday party, which was scheduled for December. I invited fifty guests for dinner at a country club. It was fabulous, and what made it more so was that Bob got to announce his new job at KPMG. All his worries about working in a new environment soon vanished, and he consistently exceeded his personal sales goals in each subsequent quarter.

During this same period, I volunteered to teach art appreciation to elementary students in our school district via a nonprofit organization, Art Goes to School. Beginning in January, the AGTS volunteers spent one week in each of the ten elementary schools within the West Chester School District, bringing some of the world's most outstanding art to the classrooms. There was also a Children's Portfolio Program featuring the artwork of students in our area and an awards ceremony celebrating the talent and diversity of the students. I loved this program and spent seven years volunteering as one of their presenters.

My life was rich, and yet I had not reached its pinnacle. I began to write the novel I had always wanted to write. I struggled with its point of view and could never tell the story that had followed me for most of my life. I joined a writer's class and asked a nearby neighbor with an editing background if he would critique my work. These endeavors resulted in a sea of red ink on every page. I was so discouraged that I gave up on ever finishing my story.

The children in our neighborhood loved Keiko. The younger ones often asked if they could "rub on her." They liked her plentiful fur and ran toward us as we walked. Our neighbors, Connor and Eva, were especially drawn to her. When Keiko was scheduled for surgery to remove several cysts on her head and upper back, I drew a picture of what she might looked like afterward. I then promised them that her hair would grow back and she would be as lovely as ever.

We had only boarded Keiko once and vowed never to do so again. Her temperament was mild, and she accepted having other dogs stay in our home when their owners were away. Likewise, a few neighbors were willing to keep Keiko for us when needed. Our little girl became nervous when we left her at home in the evening. I hired two girls who lived nearby to babysit while we were gone. That helped relieve her anxiety as well as ours.

It was apparent that Keiko was slowing down. There is an autumn in everyone's life, but most of the time, we are unaware that it has arrived. With Keiko, that time came when she was almost fourteen. Until then, every gesture and every behavior was like a graceful dance, so well-choreographed that we failed to notice that anything was different. Each night, when we sat down for dinner, she stood beside me with her eyes fixed closely on mine. She then turned her head toward the pantry, which always meant, "Get up and get me a treat!" She stamped her little foot impatiently if I were too slow: "I mean it! Get me a treat!" Most of the time, she went to the door and silently waited for me to open it to let her out. All she had to do was lie down by her bowl, and I came over and fed her. We both knew what to expect. We had been communicating like this for years. While friends and family were smug in thinking Keiko had me trained to fetch anything she wanted, I was convinced that positive reinforcement was crucial in letting her know I understood her needs. The time had finally come when our gestures were no longer the shorthand of our daily routine; it was the only way we could communicate.

When we first learned Keiko was deaf, it seemed sudden, almost without warning, following a slight ear infection. When we looked back, it was clear that her loss of hearing had been a gradual thing, so gradual that we failed to pay attention to all of the signs. She had begun to ignore the doorbell; she had stopped barking in the pre-dawn hours on trash day and no longer seemed to notice when other dogs yapped at her on our daily walks. We assumed she had become so accustomed to these sounds that she failed to find them stimulating. It never occurred to us that she couldn't hear what was happening in her world. As time went on, we attributed her lack of response when we called her to stubbornness and old age. I had even begun to doubt that she was the brilliant creature I had always claimed her to be, and was often annoyed with her for being so dense.

It took me a while to understand what was going on. Several times, I came home and was startled when I tried to open the back door, only to bump it against Keiko, who was sound asleep. She stretched out in front of the door whenever I left the house. She wanted to know when I came home. It was her way of adapting to a world of silence.

There were also other signs that we had overlooked. Keiko didn't know if we were in the same room with her unless we were in her view. Often, she wandered throughout the house in search of us. It startled her if one of us came up behind her and patted her on the back. The silence for her had become just as frightening as a sudden, unexpected noise.

While Keiko's deafness was not life-threatening, it had diminished her quality of life. Fortunately, God gives all creatures the magnificent ability to overcome the most challenging curves that life can throw their way. Already, she was finding ways to compensate for her limitations. With our help and understanding of her needs, Keiko could continue to enjoy her life to the fullest, which I now know means "to the fullest of one's ability." In this respect, we are all created equal.

And so it was that our world became one of many gestures: the swing of an arm meant "come," an extended arm with an open hand stood for "stay," and a pat on the head was our unmistakable sign for "I love you." Keiko could no longer hear Bob when he came home from work, but as soon as he knelt beside her and gave her a tummy rub, her tail would wag. There was no guessing as to what that meant. He could hear it in his heart.

With any loss of ability due to age comes the fragile realization that we are not immortal. There is a natural order to all life. I knew that despite her hearing loss, Keiko would be just fine. All I had to do was look into her eyes, and I could understand what they were saying: "Do my listening for me, Mom." And in those eyes, I could also hear her simple trust in me shouting above the sound of silence.

"Accepting things we cannot change enables us to live our lives to the fullest of our abilities."
— Patricia Taylor Wells

We spent our vacation as usual at Maple Point in June of 2000. It was a grand time with several visitors stopping by. One evening, Keiko wandered off while we watched TV with Bob's parents in the living room. She often grew tired early and fell asleep in a dark corner while waiting for us to call it a night.

When I heard Keiko's paws clawing at the wooden steps, her short gasps of spent breath, and the jingle of her dog tags as she climbed to the second floor, my stomach began to knot. In her fifteen years, Keiko had never tried to go up the stairs at the cottage. The risers were too steep, and the treads too slick for her slippery paws. She only went to the foot of the stairs and waited for someone to carry her to bed. I couldn't even imagine what had made her attempt such a feat at her fragile age. I immediately dropped what I was doing and ran, panic-stricken, down the hall. Just as I turned the corner, her head rose above the top of the stairs. She had two more steps to go. The determination on her face was both exhilarating and terrifying. She had never looked more pleased with herself. At that moment, it was like she was dancing on a cloud. But there is always a moment, perhaps, when we must decide if a discouraging look or word from someone we love or respect will keep us from reaching our dreams. When Keiko saw the terror in my eyes, she lost her confidence and began to fall.

I stood helplessly watching as her neck rolled under her chin and her paws thrashed about in the air. My cries echoed down the stairs, startling Bob and my in-laws. There was nothing Keiko could do to save herself, and midway in her fall, she seemed to understand this. She relaxed and allowed herself to roll down the steps gently. When her fall ended, Keiko stood up and wagged her tail. I rushed to her side and checked every inch of her body for injuries, but she was unscathed. More than anything, her fall made me realize how quickly and unexpectedly life can come to an end. Whatever time she had left was a blessing. I didn't want to waste it. I thanked God that Keiko was still ours to hold, love, and care for. Second chances always come with limitations. While they allow us to hold onto what we have, they also remind us that nothing lasts forever.

In early 2001, my fifteen-year-old great-niece Halley from Texas spent a week with us. We visited Gettysburg, Lancaster, and Philadelphia. We enjoyed her visit and hoped to have another opportunity to show her other parts of the country.

"The biggest heartbreak in life is realizing that we squandered the precious time we had with someone."
— Patricia Taylor Wells

When Keiko's sixteenth birthday rolled around, her life had become a struggle. It had been almost a year since her fall. In our hearts, we knew this would be her last visit to the lake, so we wanted to make it as memorable as possible. We celebrated the day by taking her out in the boat. Keiko and I sat in the stern so she could see the passing shoreline while I held her in my lap. The sun had colored her fur a brilliant white. The wind whipped through the ruff of her neck, tickling my skin as she braced herself against my shoulder. I don't think she had ever looked as beautiful or happy as she did that day. She had reached the life expectancy age for her breed, but still looked like a young pup in some ways.

We often feared that Keiko would leave us that summer, making her last visit to Maple Point even more bittersweet than it already was. There were nights when her breathing became so faint that one of us grabbed the flashlight on the nightstand and shined it on her until we could detect the soft rise and fall of her chest. The relief we felt did not stop us from worrying that we would wake in the morning and find her gone.

By the end of summer, Keiko could no longer walk up the slight climb of our street, so we bought her a Radio Flyer wagon. Its bright red body was all metal. It had high wooden panels on all four sides and wide, all-terrain tires to keep it from tipping over. It was equipped with red interior padding for added comfort. Keiko's wagon was luxurious, and she loved it. We pulled her up the street in the wagon and let her walk back home, which she could still do. Our daily walks became enjoyable again by finding a way for Keiko to continue to enjoy life to the fullest of her abilities.

"When fate hands you a lemon, make lemonade."
— *Dale Carnegie*

On the morning of September 11, 2001, I pulled Keiko up the street in her wagon. The sky was a beautiful blue, and the sun beat down on us like golden raindrops. It was a glorious morning. I stopped briefly to talk to a neighbor on our way home. Her husband was in New York City at the NY Stock Exchange to participate in ringing the bell on behalf of Campbell Soup. Keiko grew impatient, so I put her back in the wagon and continued our journey. As soon as I walked through the door, I saw the World Trade Center engulfed in flames on the small television above the kitchen sink. I had forgotten to turn it off before leaving. Like everyone else, I assumed that a terrible accident had taken place. As I cleared the breakfast dishes, the second tower was hit. It was then that my heart filled with terror. I immediately ran to the phone and tried to call Bob. I wanted to gather everyone I loved around me. My ordinary day had become one of absolute horror, overwhelming sadness, and immense fear. I didn't know anyone who was in the Towers, the Pentagon, or on any of the four planes, but that didn't matter. It felt like I had lost a member of my family.

I gazed up at the sky when I took Keiko out that evening. It was so dark that it looked like the stars had shut their eyes in horror. There were no twinkling lights of circling aircraft waiting to land at the regional airport, no drone of engines to drown the crescendo of silence. The night air had never felt so lonely. None of us knew what would come in the morning. We could only believe that there would be one.

A hard lesson had been learned that day. It was not our homes, our cars, our money that mattered, but our families, our friends, our country. I wept for everyone who had not had the opportunity to say goodbye to those they loved. It had happened to me once, and the pain of it still lives. In truth, we should all live as if it were our last day or the last day for anyone we love. I held Keiko closer to my heart that evening than I ever had before.

For the last six months of her life, we carried Keiko up and down the stairs. We helped her stand so she could eat or drink. We lifted her from the floor whenever she needed to change positions. As the weeks passed, life became increasingly difficult for her and us. We were up three or four times a night. Our backs ached from lifting her, and we suffered from a lack of sleep. Each night, we prayed that she would leave this world gently. More than anything, we wanted it to be her decision, not ours. Autumn turned to winter. The days were short and cold, and the nights long and colder. We did everything we could to make her comfortable. And each night, we prayed that she would fly away with angels in the darkness of the night.

It was a Tuesday morning in early February when we woke, knowing the time had come to make the most painful decision of our lives. We had not discussed it or set any date, but we instinctively knew what must be done. It took me most of the day to gather enough courage to call our veterinarian. All I told the receptionist was that I was calling about Keiko. From the sound of my voice, she knew what I meant. She asked if we wanted to bring her in that evening. That was too soon for me, so I made the appointment for early Saturday morning. Those next few days were almost unbearable. We agonized over whether we had let Keiko live too long or if we were letting her go too soon.

In so many ways, Keiko had tried to tell us that her time was drawing near. She had grown weary of all our attention and hid in tight little places. Every breath Keiko took was both precious and painful. During these sacred moments, we knelt beside her and ran our hands softly down the center of her back. Then, without practice or learning, and in voices that were not even our own, we spoke to her in ancient, spiritual whispers, words to help her on her journey, words that expressed the wisdom of the ages, the sanctity of all life, and the knowledge that everything must come full circle. But always, just as her breathing had faded into nothingness, a single tear would roll from her eye. She was unable to let go of the love between us.

Several neighbors dropped by during the week to say goodbye to Keiko. Some brought calla lilies, and others, especially the children, just wanted to pet her one last time. One neighbor brought a fluffy white woolen blanket, symbolic of Keiko's soft, beautiful coat. All of their gestures were deeply touching.

Still, Saturday morning came, and with it came the burden of routine. We carried Keiko down the stairs, stood outside with her in the morning chill, and helped her stand while she ate breakfast. Afterward, we held her for as long as possible, knowing that these precious moments would have to last a lifetime.

Bob wrapped Keiko in her blanket and placed her on my lap for the somber ride to the veterinary clinic. My heart ached as she leaned her head against my chest. It seemed so unjust to end her life, so unmerciful not to end it. We were ushered into an examination room upon arrival at the clinic. It was the same one we had been in many times before. I had expected someplace holier.

We sat in the chairs along the wall. Keiko lay in Bob's lap with her head resting on one of his arms. Looking deeply into her eyes, I pondered the age-old question: Do animals have souls? Some do, I think, especially dogs. Why else would we fall in love with puppies, allow them to live in our homes, and then weep so bitterly when they are gone? Unlike humans, they don't seek God or wrestle with who they are. They come into this world knowing how to live. They understand the meaning of their lives and accept what is, even their mortality, in the simplest terms. Perhaps that is the purest ambition of every soul.

When our veterinarian entered the room, I could tell she had been crying. Knowing she had not grown too accustomed to this part of her job was comforting. She explained what would happen quietly and asked if we wanted to be with Little Girl until the end. We could not imagine it any other way. She carried Keiko out of the room to insert a catheter in her leg. When they returned, the veterinarian placed Keiko on the cold, steel examining table. Keiko began to panic. I wanted to call the whole thing off. After she had calmed down, I placed her blanket under her to keep her from sliding. Bob held onto her as he bent over and whispered in her ear the love that only she could understand. I sank to my knees beside the table. As I held her front paws, our eyes met for the last time.

It took only five seconds to end her life. She passed quickly and gently. Her little eyes closed, and she lay her head on her paws. And then, in the tenderest expression imaginable, a single tear rolled from her eye. We all wept.

We couldn't bear to go home afterward. Instead, we drove to Lancaster, where we walked around pretending that it was just an ordinary day. We ate lunch and finally returned to West Chester. I cried when we entered our empty house, uncertain if my tears would stop or if I could ever love another dog as much as I loved Little Girl.

Keiko didn't fly away with angels in the darkness of the night. She left us on a bright, beautiful Saturday morning, just like the one when she had arrived in our home years ago. We loved her more than anything. We always will. If she is looking down from heaven, I hope she understands. I hope she knows we never wanted to do this, that it was only our great love for her that allowed us to end her suffering. I hope she knows that she will always live on in our hearts. I truly believe God wouldn't make these magnificent creatures our best friends if he intended to bar them from heaven.

"And I believe that angels breathe,
And that love will live on and never leave."
— Richard Marx/Linda Thompson

To say we miss Keiko is an understatement. She is just as absent from our lives as anyone we have loved and lost. I thank God for the unconditional love that she gave us, which, over time, helped restore the sense of well-being we had lost in that single, terrifying moment when our home was invaded. We learned to love, laugh, and live without fear through Keiko. We also learned the heartbreak of loving and the undeniable transience of all life. It was no mistake that she found her way into our lives.

Loss is a personal matter and can only be measured by those who experience it. Almost immediately after Keiko's passing, people asked us if we would get another puppy. It was a painful question that suggested she could be easily replaced. However, the silence of those who knew how important Keiko was in our lives hurt us the most. Because we spend more meaningful time with our pets than with people, their loss can be deeply wounding. We all feel uneasy and even vulnerable in the presence of someone who has suffered a loss. A simple hug or pat on the hand is all it takes to express compassion. Dogs are good at this. They always know when to rest their chin on someone's knee.

We have always felt that our world was extraordinary because of Keiko. She was with us for so long that we seldom stopped to think how precious our time together was. Now, she is not there to greet me when I walk through the door. There is an emptiness that follows me from room to room. Until she was gone, I was never aware of how much her presence filled the space in my life. I miss the impatient sigh each morning that let me know it was time to take her out. I miss the tender moment of every evening when she curled up on her bed and closed her eyes like a sleeping angel. I miss bending over and kissing her on the nose. I miss saying to Bob as I watched her dream, "Look at the Little Girl." I miss seeing that same sweet pose that never failed to touch my heart or make taking care of her seem less of a burden and more of a reward. Keiko was the sweetest, loveliest creature I had ever known. She will live in our hearts forever.

Farewell, Little Girl, farewell.

HALO'S STORY

October 1, 2001 — August 14, 2014

WE WAITED SIX months before considering getting another dog. Time had not lessened the thought of losing Keiko. I asked a neighbor if I could walk her dog, Maggie, each morning. Her hands were full with her two young sons, so she was delighted about my offer. Maggie, a Golden Retriever, had stayed in our home several times when her family was away. She and Keiko had gotten along well. At night, Maggie crawled under our bed to sleep. We often wondered how she managed to squeeze between the mattress frame and the floor. Since Keiko was deaf, nothing bothered her much, so we let Maggie sleep where she wanted.

Walking with Maggie was therapeutic for me. I liked being in the calm of nature. We had a large herd of deer that frequented a wooded lot along our route. Once, when walking downhill, two deer jumped over our heads from one side of the road to the other. Even though I was startled, I was also amazed. Maggie remained calm and did not bark despite our close call of being clobbered by the sharp hoofs of the deer.

I eventually stumbled across the phone number of an American Eskimo breeder in Philadelphia. Steve was also a member and former president of the American Eskimo Dog Fanciers of Greater Philadelphia. Bob and I had decided we wanted two female Eskies and had already named them "Angel" and "Chloe." We couldn't wait to find the perfect matches we longed for.

I was a bit nervous about calling the breeder. I was afraid I was not ready to have another dog. No one, not even the two females I envisioned, could take Keiko's place in my heart. Besides, I didn't

"Once you have had a wonderful dog, a life without one is a life diminished."
— Dean Koontz

know that much about the breeder. I started to hang up when a soft-spoken man answered my call. He listened patiently to what I was seeking, but then crushed me completely by telling me he would not, under any circumstances, sell two female Eskies to me. I didn't know what to say or think. Steve explained that two female dogs in the same household would often "fight to the finish" if they didn't get along. He said he would sell me two male dogs or a male and a female dog, but not two females. However, he told me he had no dogs ready to sell besides a ten-month-old male he had rescued from the family that bought him. Steve said the family, who lived in New York City, had kept the dog locked in a kennel outside their apartment all day while they were at work. The dog was bored and received little attention from his owners. He also spent the night in the kennel, which, although brought inside, kept him away from the family. Steve checked on new owners, especially if things didn't seem right. Sometimes, he sought out neighbors who might have noticed how the new owner was treating the dog.

As much as I felt bad for this dog, he wasn't what Bob and I were looking for as a pet. Steve suggested that we attend an annual picnic for American Eskimo Dogs sponsored by the American Eskimo Dog Fanciers of Greater Philadelphia, which took place in July. He said there would be numerous breeders and their dogs at the event. I could hear a dog barking in the background, which I assumed was the ten-month-old wanting attention. I told Steve I would think about it, but I doubted I would get back in touch with him.

When I told my friend Debbie about the picnic, she insisted that Bob and I go there. Not only that, she wanted to go, too. I had met Debbie a year ago when I walked into the gift shop she owned in downtown West Chester. What got my attention was the fluffy white dog asleep in a basket at the checkout counter. Debbie introduced me to "Precious," who happened to be a part miniature Eskie. We were both excited about this and soon began dog-sitting for each other. Debbie and her husband lived downtown in a historic Victorian house near the gift shop. We had many things in common besides our love of Eskies.

Debbie brought Precious to the picnic. When we arrived, I felt overwhelmed by the number of American Eskimos kept on leashes or in temporary outdoor dog pens. From a distance, they all looked alike. I asked someone to point Steve out so I could meet him. Steve was a large man with a bald head, which did not fit my description of what he looked like based on his gentle voice during our telephone conversation. After we were introduced, Steve asked if I would hold onto the dog he had with him for a few minutes. I agreed and asked for the dog's name. Although I was surprised at his name, "Halo," it suited him. He was perfectly behaved and was one of the most gorgeous dogs I had ever seen. My only disappointment was that he didn't pay much attention to me. It was hard to believe this was the ten-month-old rescue dog Steve had told me about. But it didn't matter. Halo was not the dog we were looking for, and we still preferred to have two females. With that, we came back home empty-handed.

For the next week, I couldn't stop thinking of Halo. Whenever I mentioned him, Bob reminded me of all the potential problems buried inside him. Raising a dog is difficult enough, so why take on more than we could handle? I reminded Bob that Halo was so handsome, and at the picnic, he was well-behaved. I insisted that we see Halo one more time. I needed to determine for myself whether he was right for us. Bob reluctantly agreed. I contacted Steve, and we scheduled an appointment for Saturday at his mother's house.

Steve's mother opened the door and led us to the patio in the backyard. A few minutes later, Steve appeared with Halo, who was sparkling clean. Halo checked us out and even placed his paws on our knees, which I interpreted as acceptance of us. He seemed like a healthy, happy dog. We knew on the spot that we wanted Halo, so Steve began processing the contract he had already prepared.

Halo's pedigree was very impressive. His sire was WhiteLight's Stardust Imji, and his dam was HRH Princess Taphene. We decided to keep his birth name, WhiteLight's Halo. "WhightLight" refers to the registration name the breeder, Steve, gave his puppies. We were glad to learn that even if we neutered Halo, he still maintained his purebred status. However, some dog shows do not allow neutered dogs to participate if they are judged on breeding stock to determine desirable traits, health, and breed standards.

We never had an opportunity to meet Stardust Imij, but Steve's images of him were gorgeous beyond belief. Halo inherited many of his features.

We had brought a dog kennel with us, just in case. Halo was fine until we started driving away. He barked frantically and nonstop. Bob pulled off the road and stopped the car. I got in the back seat and opened the kennel door so I could hold Halo for the rest of our ride home. That seemed to calm him.

We first put Halo in the backyard instead of taking him into the house. We took off his leash so he could explore his new home. We had bought a Frisbee for him to play with, but he didn't seem interested. Halo mainly sat and looked around. It took time for him to adjust, but we were confident that we could help him through the process. When we went inside, Halo found a floor vent next to the wall to lie on. He liked the cool air blowing under his belly.

Not long after we had Halo, we neutered him since we never intended to breed or show him. Wearing a silly plastic cone on his head was something all dogs dreaded. We were all glad when he could take it off.

Soon after that ordeal, Halo became the dominant member of our household. Halo considered anyone who came close to us a threat, whether dog or human. From what we understood, defensive behavior was Halo's method of survival. He quickly developed a bad reputation in our neighborhood. The more people became afraid of him, the more I was determined to love him till he felt safe.

Not long after he had been with us, Halo's breeder, Steve, contacted us and asked if he could visit us. The owner of one of Halo's sisters would also like to meet us. Mary Jo and her husband, Steve, lived in Elizabethtown, about sixty-eight miles from West Chester. I worried that Halo would not make a good impression and that Steve would want to take him back from us. I also didn't know what to expect when Halo met his sister. Would he remember her? Or what if he was aggressive toward her?

All my concerns disappeared once Mary Jo and Steve arrived. Halo was exuberant upon seeing his sibling, and Steve's presence kept him calm and obedient. Halo was like a new dog altogether.

The biggest surprise, however, was learning that Halo's litter included him and two females, Angel and Chloe. I couldn't believe it. These were the same names Bob and I had chosen for the initial female puppies we had wanted. Life is certainly unexpected. I can only explain this consequence intuitively. We felt privileged that Angel and Chloe were Halo's sisters.

Halo's first meeting with Angel certainly was not his last. Mary Jo and Steve were as happy as we were to let our Eskies get together as often as possible. Mary Jo liked to dress Angel up in royal robes and various costumes. She presented Halo with a tuxedo outfit that made him even more handsome than he already was.

Out of the presence of Mary Jo, her husband Steve, and our breeder Steve, Halo's behavior grew steadily worse. He was vicious toward anyone he didn't know. People feared him, so we had to keep him on a tight leash to prevent him from biting someone, especially the children, who always wanted to pet him until they got too close, and he scared them. The looks we got from the parents in our neighborhood made us feel like we had no business having a dog if we couldn't control him.

There were "bad" things Halo did that made us laugh. Not long after we adopted Halo, I noticed that the tablecloth in the dining room was frequently wrinkled. There was no doubt this was Halo's doing. I assumed he was trying to reach something, although there was nothing but a centerpiece to entice him, and even that didn't seem likely. One day, as I walked down the stairs across from the dining room, I was startled to see Halo asleep on top of the table. I was surprised that he could jump over the backs of the chairs without pushing them out of the way, which would have made a loud enough sound for me to catch him in the act. He didn't try to hide his mischievous deed, and as I observed him, I determined he was jumping up on the table because he wanted to look outside the windows facing the front of the house. Soon, I found a cushioned bench that he could easily jump on and see everything there was to see. Still, I didn't trust him. I removed the tablecloth and sprinkled white flour on the pads that protected the wood table. I would know if Halo was still jumping on it by the footprints he left behind. After a week, I wiped off the flour and replaced the tablecloth.

Halo was also notorious for stealing food out of my hands while I was preparing dinner. He could stretch his neck far enough to reach anything within his range. And once he had hold of something, he could run off without worrying about being caught.

More and more, it became apparent that Bob and I were not well-suited for a high-strung dog that was totally in charge of its affairs.

In addition to visiting us occasionally, Steve encouraged us to join the American Eskimo Dog Fanciers of Greater Philadelphia club. We enjoyed meeting other Eskie parents and hoped to learn

> *"All my dogs have been scamps and thieves and troublemakers, and I've adored them all."*
> — *Helen Hayes*

from their experience regarding Halo's behavior. Steve also invited us to a specialty dog show limited to American Eskimo dogs. Not only was Halo's dam one of the participants, but Steve said we could bring Halo with us. Of course, that meant keeping him from acting up. According to Steve, Halo needed more socialization, and what better place than a dog show? Before the show began, Steve asked me if I would handle Halo's dam, Taphene. Steve had problems with his feet, which were causing him great pain. I was unprepared for this, but Steve insisted I take his place. He told me to do whatever the judges said. Surprisingly, showing a dog wasn't difficult since the dogs participating in this activity were well-trained and obedient. Despite how awkward I felt, I was delighted that Taphene placed third in her class.

The focus of dog shows is the dog's physical appearance and structure rather than its obedience or agility. Often, breeders show their dogs to determine if they meet purebred standards. Every win elevates a dog to higher levels, which may eventually lead to competing in the Best of Show for their breed. Aside from helping breeders determine the likelihood that a particular dog will achieve championship status, dog shows also promote responsible breeding.

At least Halo behaved pretty well. That may have been due to Steve's presence. I was glad he didn't bark like one of the other dogs in the audience throughout the show. The judges and handlers were annoyed and didn't hesitate to show their displeasure, as evident from the expressions on their faces.

Later, we were invited to another Eskie event, this time outdoors. It was a beautiful day, and seeing a row of fluffy white dogs up against a blue sky was breathtaking. Owners had plenty of space to walk their dogs and run behind them as long as they were kept on a leash. There was also a costume parade. Mary Jo loaned Angel's royal robe and crown for Halo to wear. She dressed Angel in a pink princess dress, which suited her perfectly. And while Halo seemed to enjoy these activities, he was not yet trustworthy among other dogs or people who were strangers to him. Like many rescued dogs, Halo had formed a strong bond with Bob and me. But if anyone came into our home or got too near him on our walks, he growled and barked fiercely. He considered himself our protector. Undoubtedly, he had picked up cues from us dating back to the home invasion in Houston. Like Keiko, Halo sensed how stressed we became when the doorbell rang. We had carried this trauma with us for many years. It was time to look for a trainer to help us.

Initially, we enrolled Halo in an introductory puppy training class at PetSmart. He did fine and was awarded a graduate cap. Afterward, he received an award for passing the intermediate class.

Later, I found a young woman named Laura who came to our house to help us with Halo. She also suggested that we take Halo *"Dogs like to obey. It gives them security."* — *James Herriot* to a daycare service near us. I was initially reluctant, but soon found that dropping him off at this open-air facility allowed me worry-free time for myself. The kennel workers kept the dogs together in a large, fenced, concrete outdoor area. There was also a shed where the dogs could go in case of rain. I was always amazed that the dogs took naps together each afternoon. Any dog that misbehaved was quickly corrected. But no matter how much training Halo received, he continued to test the boundaries with his aggression toward anyone who came near us.

Someone told me about a trainer who worked with difficult dogs. I called him and made an appointment for him to come to our home one evening. He asked that we keep Halo out of sight shortly before he arrived for our session. The trainer, Tom, asked us to stand in the hallway once we released Halo. Initially, Halo growled viciously at Tom, who quickly ended Halo's aggression. In less than a minute, Halo was calm and obedient. It was a miracle that I found difficult to believe. Tom walked all around me, but Halo maintained his good demeanor. We went outside so that Tom could release the two dogs he had brought for the second phase of our session. Halo was on a leash but maintained his position without getting overly excited. We knew, of course, that this was not the end of Halo's problems, but it was reassuring to know that we could learn how to deal with them.

Tom owned and operated a dog kennel in Coatesville, Pennsylvania, about thirty miles from us. Bob and I drove to Wonmanog Kennels the following weekend to check it out. We both wondered if any dogs were staying there since we didn't hear any barking. The place was out in the country and was both pleasant and quiet. A large wooden sign painted with the kennel's name featured a white circle with a malamute dog in its center. "Wonmanog" was the name of the kennel itself. Although it was not a direct translation of "happy days," which was the name of the owner's daycare program, it seemed to convey the idea of a fun and positive experience for pets.

It was after five o'clock. Customers had already picked up their dogs or cats that day, and no pets were playing outside. As we followed Tom into the kennels, we were amazed. All the cages were filled with quiet, obedient, and happy dogs. Tom had been a drill sergeant in the U.S. Army, which made me wonder if all the pets were afraid of him. Yet, it was apparent that none of the dogs were anxious around him. They watched Tom and listened to every word he said. His presence, I determined, was what kept them quiet.

Another interesting aspect of Tom's life was that he owned and trained a team of Alaskan Malamute dogs. He drove his dogs to Alaska every year to participate in the Iditarod. Malamutes are known for their power to carry heavy loads rather than their speed. However, mushers often form strong bonds with their dogs and vice versa. Their relationship is frequently characterized by mutual trust, affection, and appreciation of their accomplishments.

From then on, we boarded Halo anytime we were going away from home and gave him frequent daycare visits at Wonmanog. It was a big help knowing I didn't have to worry about Halo when I was away from him.

Tom and his son, who also worked at the kennel, had grown fond of Halo. Even so, often, they displayed their disappointment in me for not having more control over Halo's behavior. I loved Halo with all my heart. But that was not enough.

One evening in late spring, Bob and I sat on our deck to enjoy a glass of wine and a comfortable breeze before the sun went down. Halo spread out between our feet as he listened to varieties of thrushes, sparrows, and warblers begin the "dusk chorus" typical of many bird species.

My favorite time of the day was soon interrupted by a loud whooshing sound. I looked up and saw nothing on either side of me. Again, there was a whoosh. I turned around, startled to see a hot air balloon descending in the sky behind me. It drifted slowly to my right. The pilot and his four passengers, whose faces we could now see, waved at us from their wicker basket without much concern about how close they were to us. Halo began barking, and we started shouting for the pilot to raise his altitude. Our interaction with the pilot and passengers had suddenly become less friendly.

The balloon was near our roof structure, about ten feet above our driveway. The distance between our house and the next-door house was approximately twenty feet. The balloon was dangerously close to us. We screamed at the pilot to move away. According to the U.S. Federal Aviation Administration (FAA), aircraft, including balloons, are forbidden to get closer than five hundred feet to any person, vessel, vehicle, or structure unless due to an emergency or when landing. In congested areas like our neighborhood, the restriction is much higher. We wondered what the pilot intended, grateful that the balloon had floated away from our house and was in the process of landing on the street next to a vacant lot. We rushed toward the balloon, hanging onto Halo by his leash. A few neighbors came outside with their children, excited to see the balloon. Rather than apologizing, the pilot smirked at our claim that he could have burned our house down, injured us, or his passengers. He went out of his way to make us look foolish. I filed a claim against the FAA. It was no surprise that the charges were dismissed by one of the pilot's buddies, who somehow managed to be in charge of the investigation. The only reason the pilot landed the balloon in the street was so he could claim that he was not in violation of FAA rules. Although I was disappointed with the findings, continuing my complaint wasn't worth the effort.

Halo soon forgot about the balloon and returned to barking at birds flying high in the air. I noticed how he chased them from the ground, especially large-winged fowls like eagles or flocks of geese. I wondered what he thought about the giant balloon. To him, it was probably just another big bird soaring in the sky. Halo also jumped at any airplane passing overhead. Most likely, this was because his initial owner kept him outside in a cage all day. Watching planes and birds was his sole form of entertainment.

We always enjoyed being around Mary Jo, Steve, and Angel whenever possible. We hadn't heard from Steve, the breeder, since the American Eskimo picnic we hosted in our backyard a few weeks before. As a precaution, we hired Laura to assist us in managing Halo if needed. Steve brought Taphene, and Mary Jo and her husband were there with Angel. It was a fun day, and we even got a few photos of all the American Eskimos present lined up on top of the slope in our backyard. The one thing I regretted about adopting Halo when he was ten months old was that I didn't have any baby pictures of him other than a single black and white photo Steve found and gave to me. I still treasure it.

Shortly after the picnic, Laura and her husband announced they were moving to Austin, Texas. I was so disappointed. I created a farewell card for Laura, loaded with pictures of Halo, and wrote a poem full of accolades to accompany it. In particular, Laura showed Halo how to find comfort when stressed by lying on his elevated dog bed.

Although it had been a year and a half since we adopted Halo, we had not taken him to Keuka Lake, where Bob's parents, Lee and Barbara, owned a summer cottage. We had already visited my in-laws early in the summer before we got Halo in August 2002. In 2003, we had planned a sixtieth wedding anniversary party for Bob's parents. Since numerous family and friends would be attending the event, we decided that Halo would be better off at Wonmanog Kennels. It was too soon to introduce my in-laws to him.

Living in Philadelphia made driving to the Finger Lakes more than once a year easy. Bob's Uncle Frank, who lived in Canandaigua, New York, passed away in June 2004. We drove up without Halo for his funeral.

We finally got to bring Halo along on our second trip to the lake in late June. There was much going on in our lives that summer.

We had just put our house in West Chester for sale. Bob, who had worked for the accounting firm KPMG since early 1998, was being transferred at our request to Atlanta, where we had lived ten years ago. Although we loved West Chester and all our neighbors, we were tired of the snow, and I wanted to be closer to my parents. My father had fallen the year before and broken his hip. Sometime later, he became seriously ill. I flew to Texas to see him. By the time I got there, my father had been given six hours to live. A Catholic priest, who appeared to be from India, suddenly showed up and asked if he could pray over my father. My father survived, but we never saw the mysterious priest again. Although my sister lived in California, her two daughters lived in East Texas, near my parents' home in Greenville. Atlanta had not been our first choice for a transfer, but it was the only job opening KPMG had at the time relevant to Bob's work credentials.

Of course, we were unhappy that soon, we would no longer be that close to Keuka Lake. Everything in life is a tradeoff at one time or another. For now, we only wanted to enjoy Halo at the lake. His first meeting with Lee and Barbara took us by surprise. He did not act up or growl at them. We were certain Halo had never gone swimming, so we bought him a bright red life jacket with black trimming. He loved it but didn't seem too interested in swimming. We put the jacket on him anyway, as he seemed very proud when wearing it. Like Keiko, Halo enjoyed riding in the boat on Keuka Lake. Often, he sat next to Bob at the helm, but most of the time, he preferred sitting in the stern, where I usually sat, as it offered a smoother ride during rough water.

That summer, I realized how much I loved Halo. I never thought I could love another dog as much as I loved Keiko, but the proof was there. Halo and I had bonded, and no one could take that away from us.

One day, shortly after our trip, I was walking across the family room when a news report on TV caught my attention. I listened intently as the reporter detailed the deplorable conditions of fourteen American Eskimo dogs living in a rowhouse in Philadelphia. To my horror, the breeder involved in this incident was Steve. I immediately contacted Mary Jo to see if she knew anything about this. We both wondered how this could be true.

There was also a *Philadelphia Daily News* magazine article regarding the warrant for access to Steve's rowhouse, where the dogs were kept in unimaginable filth. Additionally, a story was featured in the Philadelphia SPCA Newsletter. Both articles were enough to make you sick. And yet, my mind could not accept what I was reading.

Even more alarming, this event did not suddenly appear. The situation being investigated had been ongoing for six years. Despite the neighbor's complaints about barking dogs most of the night and foul odors, Steve had always refused to allow anyone to inspect his rowhouse. Without entry, there was never enough evidence to file charges against him. Finally, a neighbor granted the SPCA officer access to peer over her fence into Steve's backyard. The officer saw all he needed to serve a search warrant. The fourteen American Eskimos were removed from the premises and taken to the SPCA, where they would be cared for and made available for adoption if the court ruled against Steve. Five of the dogs had been living outdoors without shelter. Their fur was matted and filthy. They drank contaminated water from a child's swimming pool. The house itself was declared uninhabitable. There were cockroaches, rats, flies, garbage, and animal waste everywhere. The dogs were being fed, but that was about the only care they received.

Steve did not resist the warrant to search his home. Nor was he anywhere in sight when the SPCA officers burst open the door. His house was cleaned and sealed a few days later, and Steve was forced to stay with friends or family and rounded up the dogs. They found Steve sitting on the bed in his upstairs bedroom. He remained calm throughout the process while waiting for his hearing regarding cruelty to animals charges held against him.

But the story did not end there. Mary Jo and I were not the only members of Steve's circle who began calling the reporter who wrote the article about the fourteen American Eskimo dogs. We were astounded and certain that this was not the Steve we knew, whose dogs, in public, were impeccably clean and groomed, totally obedient, and calm around other dogs and people. None of this made sense. Steve had been in our home several times, usually when Mary Jo and Angel visited us. We frequently communicated with him by email or phone. The reporter had difficulty understanding how dog lovers like us were not outraged about the treatment the Eskies endured under Steve's care. From the reporter's point of view, Steve was a monster. For those who knew Steve, this situation was only conceivable had Steve developed a recent medical condition or injury that impaired his thinking.

I wanted everyone to know that there was a different side to Steve. I sent the reporter a photograph I took at the Eskie picnic Bob and I hosted a while back, featuring Angel, Steve, Halo, and Taphene sitting on a bench in our backyard. The photo was included in a follow-up article about the case. By then, even the reporter had realized there was nothing clear-cut about why Steve, a former president of the local American Eskimo Club, kept the dogs he loved in such horrific circumstances. And how did he manage to do so without any of his buyers finding out? Steve was very strict when it came to selling one of his dogs. Buyers had to sign a detailed contract loaded with dos and don'ts. They never saw Steve's rowhouse. Instead, he always met prospective customers at one of his family members' homes. Bob and I thought it was strange when Steve showed us Halo at his mother's home. He claimed that showing a dog away from his other purebreds was easier.

But still, why didn't Steve reach out for help? For one, he was too overwhelmed to take control of his situation. Others like Mary Jo and I do not dispute Steve's love for his Eskies, despite how that may sound.

Bob and I moved to Atlanta a few months later. I never saw or spoke to Steve again. I don't know the outcome of his hearing. I feel terrible about what happened to him. All I could think of was that had we not adopted Halo, he would have been inside the rowhouse with the fourteen American Eskimos. Of course, sadly, he had been there.

I sometimes wonder if we made the right decision about moving from Pennsylvania. There were so many memories that I would never forget. Some of our neighbors put together a scrapbook filled with photos and farewell letters. I still treasure it and occasionally thumb through it when I feel lonely or uncertain.

We rented an apartment in Atlanta while our house was being built. Since we were closer to my parents following our move, we traveled to Texas for Thanksgiving. Halo could go with us since we were driving to and from Greenville. During this time, my cousin Virginia's battle with cancer had escalated. I regret that we couldn't see her while we were in Texas. Soon after we returned to Atlanta, her brother Stephen called one evening to tell us she would probably not be with us much longer. 2004 marked the beginning of a long trail of sorrow.

When the phone rang again, I was almost too afraid to answer it. Bob and I were sitting on the sofa with Halo between us. The person who was calling identified himself as the sheriff of a small county in Pennsylvania.

Trouble seemed to follow Halo everywhere he went. After the sheriff determined that we were the persons he sought, he asked if we were missing a dog. His question startled me. I told the officer that our dog was sitting next to us. He then asked for our pet's name and inquired about its breed, age, color, and sex. I was reluctant to give him any more information. The sheriff explained that someone had found a small, white dog near the county landfill. The dog was wearing one of Halo's expired dog tags. I told the sheriff that we had recently moved to Atlanta. He had tracked us down via the information on the tag and the County Treasurer's office. Since we had forwarded our phone number, he could call us. I remembered having thrown Halo's old tags in the trash before moving. It never occurred to me that someone would find them in the trash dump and use them on their dog, but they did. It was strange to know that a stolen identity wasn't limited to humans.

The following week, Virginia passed away. Ironically, my cousin Terri's husband also died on the same day. Both of them had been

"Be the person your dog thinks you are."
— C.J. Frick

receiving treatment at M.D. Anderson in Houston. I drove back to Texas for Virginia's funeral, leaving Bob to care for Halo. It was a sad time for my family, with more to come. Not long after, Stephen's wife, who had also been very ill, passed away. All three of the deceased were taken too soon. The loss of someone young is perhaps the saddest thing we will ever face. When I returned to Atlanta, I promised to stay in touch with family and friends as much as possible.

While we were still living in the apartment, Bob went downstairs one morning to take Halo out for a walk. Our apartment was located on the second floor, but the stairway was enclosed, and the bottom step led directly to the outside. Bob and Halo were surprised when they saw a man lying against the door. Not sure if the man was dead or alive, Bob shut the door and ran upstairs to call the police and the apartment manager.

Before the police arrived, the man woke up and moved off the porch. After looking through the peephole, Bob decided the man had left, and it was safe to take Halo out. The man was walking away as quickly as he could, but when he heard Halo barking, he turned around and threatened to beat Bob and his dog up if they came any closer. I'm pretty sure that the man was no match for Halo. He was long gone by the time the police arrived. They assumed he was a homeless alcoholic due to the wine and beer bottles he left behind. He likely had come through the back gate across from us, which apartment residents, including Bob, used for boarding MARTA, Atlanta's Rapid Transit Authority.

It was late spring in 2005 before we could move into our new home. We had reunited with our friends Janis and Paul, whom we had known when we first lived in Atlanta. We went to the same Unity Church as they did, but best of all, they were willing to take care of Halo if we were out of town. It was the most worry-free arrangement I could imagine.

We were hardly settled when Bob's parents announced they were selling Maple Point. They suggested we visit the Finger Lakes in early June to help them with the sale and determine who wanted what from the cottage. Now that we were in Atlanta, we hadn't planned to take Halo with us when we visited Mapil Point. Even though Bob could only take a short time away from work, we drove to Keuka Lake with Halo. Bob then flew home while Halo and I stayed to help his parents. Later, Bob flew back to the lake for our return drive home.

Just like the year before, Halo behaved well around Lee and Barbara. However, I had to take him on a walk or drive whenever someone came to view the house. When Bob's brother and sister-in-law, Lee III and Alicia, announced they were coming to the cottage, I decided it would be best to board Halo for a few days. Lee and Barbara recommended a place where they had taken their former dog, Maggie. That summer was unusually hot, and Halo did not like sleeping in an outdoor kennel for three nights. When I picked him up at the end of his stay, he became aggressive toward the kennel owners, who were startled since he had not displayed hostility while in their care.

My next challenge was introducing Halo to Lee III and Alicia, which I expected would not go well. While Alicia wasn't bothered much by Halo's aggression, Lee III was. I had to keep Halo away from him for the rest of their visit. I was glad when Bob returned to Maple Point in a few days. Altogether, Halo and I had been there for over a month.

There were many moments I remembered from the summers we had spent on Keuka Lake. I couldn't even imagine how difficult it was for Lee and Barbara to let go of this magnificent place. Maple Point will live in all of our hearts for the rest of our lives.

On the last day of his visit, Lee III sat on a bench on the front porch, reading the newspaper. He was the most relaxed I had seen him. Suddenly, Halo jumped up on the bench and sat next to him. Lee III wasn't rattled at all, and Halo was equally calm. Maple Point had always brought healing to my life; now, it was doing the same for Lee III and Halo.

Once we were back home, we got to know some of our neighbors. They weren't the same as those in West Chester. I could tell they never would be.

I tried not to let this bother me, but it did. I was glad to have Halo to help me adjust to my new surroundings.

Atlanta was a big city. Traffic was heavy, and people were always in a hurry. And things that should have been simple to fix often became an even bigger problem. Soon after we had moved into our new home, our mail stopped being delivered. I was expecting my new driver's license, new credit cards, and an income tax refund. When I sought help from the Postal Service, things went haywire. My missing mail was at the Post Office, but the clerk would not hand it over to me since I did not have an identity card with my current address. I pointed out that she was holding the card in her hand, but she still wouldn't give it to me. She insisted it would be mailed and placed in my mailbox that afternoon. When the mailman came in the late afternoon, he passed my postbox without delivering any mail to it.

To make matters worse, the U.S. Treasury would not place a hold on my tax refund. Instead, I had to wait until the check was cashed before they could issue a new one. It took several months for everything to be taken care of. I think Halo sensed my frustration. And while he made me feel calmer, he had also become more protective and didn't want anyone near me.

After a while, I noticed things about our neighborhood that didn't seem right. Unknown to most of us, the developer had gone bankrupt and could not be found. One of the more affluent neighbors had taken over the Homeowners Association without notifying anyone. And while he was ensuring that all expenses were paid, he was also spending money on improvements that HOA members had not authorized.

In the process, the legal name for our neighborhood, which was registered with the Secretary of State of Georgia, had expired. Soon after, a neighborhood association with the same name took over the registration. I decided it was time to gather all the residents for a meeting to vote on an official Board of Directors, Bylaws, Rules and Regulations, Budgeting, and Assessments.

Once that was behind us, new issues developed. Of course, the man who unofficially took over the HOA won the vote for President of the Board. He wasted no time convincing the majority of residents that a gated community was essential for our neighborhood's security, especially since several burglaries had occurred nearby.

But not so fast; some of us cried. We needed more information, especially regarding the cost. Numerous issues had not been examined. We decided to hold a neighborhood meeting to discuss the pros and cons of converting to a gated community. We also invited a City official to address the legal issues involved.

At the time this took place, and as far as I know today, a developed community has never been converted to a gated one due to the hundred percent agreement required for property owners and mortgage lenders. There's always at least one person who votes against it. And woe to the holdouts who must live among neighbors who will carry a grudge against them.

About seven or eight households opposed having a controlled-access neighborhood. Bob and I were one of them. The ones in favor were determined to make our lives miserable. We eventually had to hire an attorney to protect our interests.

I found it difficult to be among people who seemed to have little to no common sense. Converting to a gated community is a costly endeavor. Public streets must be converted to private streets, with homeowners assuming maintenance of roads, storm sewer systems, and other infrastructure. Sometimes, the original subdivision has to be modified to accommodate access points, gates, or fencing. Maintaining a sinking fund for future expenses (especially road repairs) is also required. Most of the costs are due to the legal contracts needed between the neighborhood, emergency services, and public utilities. To live in a gated community, you must find one that already exists.

I was responsible for neighborhood security. If there was an incident, neighbors were expected to contact the appropriate emergency service (police, fire, or ambulance) and report it to me so I could advise everyone if necessary. Before long, I began receiving frequent notifications of "incidents" that didn't seem to exist once they were looked into. Interestingly, none of the events were reported to the police except for one involving our next-door neighbor.

One late afternoon, the neighbor whose wife was out of town walked down the street with a glass of wine and knocked on the door of a single woman. The neighbor asked the woman if he could look at her floor plan to see if it was the same as his. A friend was visiting the woman, so she felt okay letting him inside her house. Afterward, the woman told the neighbor that she and her friend were having dinner at another neighbor's home, so he had to leave.

When the woman and her friend returned to her house, which she had not locked, they heard the sound of running water upstairs. When they went to investigate, they were shocked to find the neighbor nude and taking a shower. The neighbor had re-entered the woman's home after she and her friend left that evening. The woman yelled for him to get out of her home. He grabbed his clothes, dressed, and ran back home. Initially, she did not call the police.

After dark, Bob saw two police cars in the neighbor's driveway when he took Halo outside. He asked one of the officers if everything was okay. The officer claimed they had everything under control. Bob, Halo, and I went upstairs to see the neighbor's driveway from the window. We opened it slightly so we could hear what was going on. The woman sat in the back seat of one of the police cars while two policemen went inside the neighbor's home to question him. They brought him outside so the woman could talk to him and decide whether to have him charged with unlawful entry and indecent exposure. Ultimately, no charges were pressed. There weren't any other crimes after that.

When the pro-gate community saw that their fake crimes were not going anywhere, they came up with a new and more sinister tactic. This time, they put all of their focus on Halo. According to one neighbor, they intended to have him declared dangerous. Halo was always on a leash or in our fenced backyard. He had never attacked or bitten anyone, but he was aggressive toward anyone he didn't know. We were very mindful about making sure he was always under our control. I decided not to walk Halo in our neighborhood. Instead, I walked him in a nearby neighborhood. We never had any problems. It was unnerving to think about how low some would stoop if anyone disagreed with their views.

In the spring of 2006, my friend Janis gave me a news clipping titled "Dog Shrink to Take on Atlanta's Flaky Fidos." Cesar Millan, commonly known as the "Dog Whisperer," was coming to town to help dog owners like me who love their pooch passionately but don't have a clue how to control them. I was very excited and was sure Halo would be a good candidate for Cesar's show, which aired each week on the National Geographic channel. Ordinarily, Cesar didn't travel far from his Dog Psychology Center in Los Angeles to film episodes of his show. But this year, he would visit six cities across the country. Atlanta would be his first stop.

Most of the time, it was the owner, not the dog, with all the problems. So, when Cesar set foot in anyone's home, he observed how they interacted. I already knew that our major problem was the doorbell. We tensed every time it rang. Despite it occurring years ago, the terror of the home invasion in Houston had followed us every step of the way.

There was much more involved than I had anticipated when it came to submitting Halo as a candidate for the *Dog Whisperer*. The production company for the show required each owner to provide a video of their dog playing or interacting with them, as well as other dogs or people, lasting between five and seven minutes. That meant buying a video camera and learning how to use it.

Everyone featured in the video had to give their consent and sign a legal document. We also had to provide information on how we heard about the dog auditions and where we obtained our dog. In addition to how old Halo was, we were asked what we knew about his history. I cringed when I saw that the entertainment company wanted to know about Halo's problems and what we had done to correct his behavior.

I felt better after being asked if there was anything unusual or funny about our dog. I noted that when Halo was proud of himself, he puffed out his chest and howled with his head held high. At times, he turned counter-clockwise circles while pivoting on his front legs as he navigated his way around the room to find the perfect spot to lie down. Halo also enjoyed watching videos of himself.

We asked Janis and her husband, Paul, if they would be willing to participate in our video. Halo became intolerable if they tried to leave after visiting our home, but other than that, he behaved pretty well around them. We also asked two of our neighbors if they would walk up to our gate with their dogs so we could film Halo acting up once he saw them.

We did not hear from the entertainment company until September. We were told that five dogs in Atlanta had been selected

"Every dog must have his day."

— Jonathan Swift

for the *Dog Whisperer*. Halo was one of them. Only three of the five selected, however, would be included in the show when it aired. Halo was designated as a backup in case any of the top three dogs had to drop out for any reason. I was both excited and disappointed. I wrote a letter back to the entertainment company, providing details that I wish I had mentioned earlier regarding Halo's behavior and what a nightmare our lives had become due to the neighborhood controversy. My letter didn't change things. I watched the episode featuring the three Atlanta dogs when it aired later on. I was sure Halo would have been a better candidate and could have benefited more from Cesar's help than the chosen dogs did. People often ask me why we keep Halo since he's so difficult to manage. For me, getting rid of him was not an option, but getting the best help for him was.

If nothing else, my video camera was used to film family and friends during the summer months while I waited to see if Halo would become a TV star. I traveled to Texas to visit my parents and attend an engagement party for my cousin Steve's son and his fiancée. Several cousins joined us to celebrate. Capturing them on film was something I appreciated for years to come. I also videotaped my father sharing some of his World War II stories. That film was somehow lost, but eighteen years later, it mysteriously reappeared, and I was able to write an award-winning short story about my father's map-making experience during the war.

"Everybody wants a solution on how to help their dogs, but we can't really see the problem until we reconnect ourselves to our instinctual self."
— Cesar Millan, The Dog Whisperer

The unity church we attended held an annual Animal Blessing every October. A certificate was awarded to each participant, bearing the pet's name, which cited their loyalty, love, companionship, and devotion. I had faith in Halo, regardless of what anyone else might think. We were on a journey together, protecting each other as we made our way through it.

Despite this, I was becoming increasingly frustrated. I was afraid to go outside with Halo. I always kept a lookout for unexpected encounters with unfriendly neighbors who might try to stage an incident to get even with us for not voting for the gated community they wanted so badly. I decided to contact a friend from Unity Church who specialized in helping horses and other animals that had experienced physical and mental trauma. Most of our meetings were remote, with Halo and me sharing soothing sessions over the phone. It was a time for us to remain calm, to express our love for one another, and to provide healing. However strange this may seem, it was invigorating.

A few weeks into our therapy, the instructor decided it would be more beneficial for me to begin a more intensive meditative form similar to Reiki. I accepted her suggestion, and from then on, I went to her studio, lay on a table, and closed my eyes with soothing music surrounding me. The technique was so relaxing that I fell into a trance. Afterward, I shared the visions I had experienced with my instructor. On one occasion, she stopped the session and asked for the name of our former dog. After giving her the name, she informed me that Keiko was in the room with us. I cannot explain this, but I felt it. Another puzzling event occurred when I entered our guest room to get something one evening. I saw Halo and wondered how he had gotten into the room. A few minutes later, Halo ran into the room, barking loudly. The dog I had initially seen was not Halo. I could only assume it was Keiko's spirit and that she was trying to convey something to me. I did not know what to believe, but I found comfort in feeling her presence. It was as though she was watching over me and preparing me for the difficult times ahead.

Bob had only been with KPMG in Atlanta for about three years when things began to fall apart. First, he had to have surgery to remove a kidney stone. Afterward, he developed a staph infection that led to sepsis, which is life-threatening. He was taken by ambulance early one morning after his fever reached as high as 105 degrees. He was hospitalized for a week and then ordered to remain at home for several days to recuperate. It was a stressful time for both me and Halo.

One evening, my next-door neighbor, Janice, called to see if her eight-year-old daughter could come over. I wondered what that was all about, but thought it best to wait until she came to find out. Bob was dressed in his pajamas and robe, lying on a wing-back recliner chair in the family room. When I opened the door, I was surprised to see my young neighbor in a pink princess dress with puff sleeves and a tulle skirt. She was carrying a tote bag filled with several books. She asked Bob if he would like to select one of the books for her to read to him. Bob carefully surveyed the books before deciding on his favorite. The "princess" sat down on the sofa and read the story Bob had chosen. She threw her single-braided blonde hair across her shoulder as she cast her eyes on the book's pages. Halo quietly jumped on the sofa next to her and watched her read. Not once did he bark. Both the patient and Halo were charmed, and neither took their eyes off the lovely "princess."

In August 2007, my father passed away. Bob and I drove to Texas for the funeral and to help my mother with the arrangements. At least my nieces were close enough to see about her most of the time. Everything felt like an endless cloud burst was hanging over our heads.

A few months later, Bob lost his only client due to a merger with another company. Although he had the largest account in KPMG's Atlanta office until now, it took a considerable amount of time to build new clients, and, most likely, several new accounts combined would not equal as much income as the single client he had lost.

Bob began seeking employment in other areas. Eventually, he accepted a job as the Director of Sarbanes-Oxley with the Tennessee Valley Authority in Knoxville. He was later promoted to a new role as Vice President of Compliance, responsible for overseeing TVA's entire compliance program. I was amazed that nuclear, mechanical, electrical, civil, and environmental engineers reported to him. His experience with utility clients and knowledge of Sarbanes-Oxley at KPMG had paid off.

Of course, all of this meant that we had to move to Knoxville. We decided not to build a home this time. Instead, we would rent an apartment until we found a pre-owned home that met our requirements. It seemed like we looked at every available house in Knoxville before we finally saw what we were looking for. There were several things we wanted to update or change before moving in. It took considerable time and effort to find painters, carpenters, electricians, plumbers, and other necessary workers, but it was well worth it. Our new home was interesting. The former children's bedroom walls were painted with decorative murals. The young boy's room included a western frontier town, complete with a general store, a bank, a hotel, and a jail. Halo especially liked the little girl's chamber, which featured a Border Collie sitting in front of a white garden gate surrounded by wildflowers and a grassy lawn. There were also colorful birds painted in several areas in the breakfast area. We decided to retain the wall art for a while. We could always paint over it, but once we did, the images were lost forever.

Even better than the murals was the wood cabin playhouse in the backyard. There was a wooden arched bridge from the patio to the cabin. The playhouse was large enough for five or so adults to stand up straight once inside. However, the door was only about four feet high, so everyone had to stoop to enter. There were two electric lamps above the green door. We later hung a plaque between them, etched with a dog's paw print and "Halo's House."

The interior was even more amazing—the walls and ceiling featured wood paneling and five windows that opened and closed. There was also an air conditioning/heating window unit and a ceiling light. I knew immediately that the old playhouse would come in handy. I knew that Halo would be reluctant to go inside, so I devised a coordinated plan to ease his concerns. I placed a comfortable folding chair in the cabin, as I expected to spend a considerable amount of time in it. I periodically coaxed Halo to come inside with me so he could get used to staying there. I opened the windows when the temperature was mild, and I also placed a radio on a small table so he could enjoy soothing music. Little by little, he relaxed when we were together. I wasn't sure how he would react if I left him in there alone.

It took a while, but eventually, I could leave Halo in his cabin for about two hours if needed. It was beneficial when repairs were required in the house or when my writer's critique group was meeting in our home.

Later, in 2008, my niece Jenny passed away. She had been ill for over a week before visiting a doctor. By then, her life was seriously threatened due to sepsis setting in. Jenny's young son, Ricky, who was serving overseas in the Marine Corps, was unaware of his mother's situation. I contacted the Red Cross in Tyler, where Jenny lived, and asked if they could locate Ricky, who was believed to be somewhere in the Middle East, most likely Afghanistan. About four hours later, I received a call from Ricky's

Commanding Officer. The CO asked me several questions before putting Ricky on the line. It was so difficult to tell him that he may not make it in time to see his mother. The hospital in Tyler suggested that he call her since it took a couple of days for him to get there. Ricky poured his heart out while talking to her, though it was doubtful that Jenny could even hear him. The hospital staff waited until Ricky finally arrived before removing her from the ventilator that had kept her semiconscious.

Halo helped me get through the rough times in my life. He understood them. I had grieved a good deal since losing my brother when he was fourteen years old. There were moments when I wondered if life was worth it. Caring for a dog assured me that it was.

In early 2009, Bob's mother, Barbara, passed away at the age of ninety. And while we missed her, it was easier to accept the loss of someone who had lived life to the fullest. For most of her life, Barbara had had a dog. She was wise, though, to make sure her dog did not outlive her. Bob's parents were already in their eighties when their last dog, Maggie, died.

Sometime after that, Halo's ligament on his hind leg ruptured. He had to have surgery to repair it. I had no idea how to keep him from injuring himself any further. I bought a metal dog crate large enough for me to sit inside with him. At night, we wrapped Halo's leash around my wrist to prevent him from jumping off the bed. It was a difficult time for him and us. Once, he got out of the crate and jumped up on a chair, then waited proudly for me to see what he had done.

In August 2009, my mother sold her house in Greenville and moved to Tyler, where my niece, Julie, lived. It had been three years since my father passed away. I was happy about the move. It took some of the burden off my shoulders. I spent six weeks in Greenville helping her move out of the house she had lived in for thirty-five years. The whole process overwhelmed her, and I was afraid that she wouldn't adjust that easily. We had found a suitable home for her very close to Julie's. After loading everything onto the moving truck, I drove Mother and her chihuahua dog in my car to Tyler. Julie's husband drove Mother's auto to her new home. I couldn't wait to get back home to Bob and Halo. Bob had arranged for someone to walk Halo outside twice a day while he was at work. I worried that Halo might think I wasn't coming back home.

I had discovered that every year carried a burden with it. 2010 was no different. In late November, I began feeling ill. I suspected I had a UTI and needed antibiotics. I didn't want to end up like my niece, so I made a same-day appointment with my doctor's nurse practitioner. The nurse took a blood sample but wanted to wait until the results were in, which could take two or three days. I was sent home despite my better judgment. When the blood work came back, the nurse prescribed antibiotics, which I began taking immediately. I made a new appointment when it appeared that the pills weren't helping. The nurse sent me home again, convinced that the antibiotics had not had enough time to work. The next evening, close to midnight, my temperature had soared to nearly 105 degrees Fahrenheit. Bob called 911, and an ambulance was sent to whisk me to the emergency room.

Poor Halo was frantic, but there wasn't much Bob could do about it. I had sepsis, just like my niece and Bob had had previously. But this was not my first encounter with this life-threatening condition. Right after Bob and I became engaged, I was also stricken with it. I spent about a week in the hospital this go around. I was so glad to be back home. That evening, December 8, I fell fast asleep. A little after three o'clock in the morning, I was awakened shortly by a loud, odd sound, but I quickly fell back to sleep.

When I woke the next morning, I was horrified by the news that greeted me. A neighbor's home had exploded during the night. The man and woman who lived in the house were blown out of their two-story windows by the blast. Several neighbors heard the explosion and initially thought a plane had crashed. Although their home was destroyed, the couple miraculously survived. Neighbors found them on the ground amid all the rubble. Sadly, their teenage son, who lived in the basement of the home, did not survive. The night before, his sister and her roommate had stopped by to see him and her parents. They had tried to persuade them to stay overnight, but the girls decided to go back to their dorm at the University of Tennessee.

A leak in the tee connection of a main gas line caused the disaster. Gas traveled into the house from an outside line, filling up the basement. When the thermostat turned on, the house exploded.

The defective tee fittings were installed on 1,500 homes between 1997 and 2001 in the West Knoxville area. Altogether, 14,000 fittings were installed during that time frame, but no one knew which homes had the same tee fitting as the one involved in the explosion. As a precaution, the gas lines of the 14,000 homes in the area were dug up and inspected.

After this happened, I smelled gas several times when walking Halo in our neighborhood. It became my mission to report my findings directly to the gas company. Homeowners were not always present or reliable, especially if they had not detected the smell themselves or thought it unlikely that another home would explode.

Another disaster was waiting for me in 2011. In mid-spring, a severe tornado outbreak occurred in the Southern, Midwestern, and Northeastern United States over three days, from April 25 to 28. It made its way to Knoxville on April 27. Bob and I put Halo on his leash so we could grab him if necessary. According to local news outlets, tornado winds and flooding were reported in nearby areas, so we expected the same.

Once the sirens sounded constantly, we huddled inside a small bathroom located on the first floor. Suddenly, we heard loud noises that sounded like our roof and perhaps our windows were being bombarded with rocks. I worried frantically about the large window over the front door. There was a shelf below it, filled with large glass pots containing artificial floral arrangements and pebbles. If that window broke, the pots and pebbles could fly across the room as dangerously as the baseball-sized hail that was hitting the roof and sides of our house.

When the storm finally ended, I realized that Halo had kept relatively calm throughout it. He trusted us, and somehow, that kept us calm as well. When we were finally able to leave our shelter, we were overwhelmed to see that the ground was covered with hailstones, making it unsafe to assess the damage, especially since it was dark outside.

After Bob left for work the next morning, I contacted a roofer to inspect our roof and gutters. I then went up to the attic, where I saw several leaks. It was late afternoon before the roofer showed up. I put Halo in our bedroom with the door closed, knowing he wouldn't like having a stranger in our house.

There was a door on the second floor that opened to the lower attic, which was mainly used for storage. To access the upper attic and inspect the leaks, it was necessary to walk up an open riser staircase. On the other side of the loft was a pull-down attic ladder that unfolded from the ceiling to the second-floor hallway. The light switch was on that side of the attic. To reach it, you had to crawl over several rows of air-conditioning ductwork in the dark.

Once the roofer and I were in the upper attic, I climbed over the ductwork so I could turn on the light. When I stepped on the floor, I felt my foot and leg give way as the pull-down ladder unfolded beneath me. Suddenly, I was holding onto the edge of the attic floor for dear life. Since the ladder was not fully extended, I was in danger that my weight would cause it to break, bringing me down with it. The roofer tried to pull me up, but couldn't. Somehow, my adrenaline kicked in, and without much effort, I pulled myself back onto the attic floor. As I lay there, I raised my head and shoulders, only to see that my ankle was badly twisted. Although I didn't feel any pain, I was well aware that I needed medical attention. I asked the roofer to call 911 and then my husband. I also asked him to go next door and get my neighbor, who was a nurse. My neighbor, Lorraine, came over immediately, followed by an ambulance and a fire truck. By the time Bob got home, the attic was crowded with two paramedics, four firemen,

Lorraine, the roofer, and another neighbor who had heard about the incident.

The only thing I was concerned about was Halo. I was sure he was unnerved by all the unknown voices he had heard during the past hour. I asked Bob to look after him since I had plenty of help in the attic.

Getting me out of the attic was a difficult task. The rescue crew members decided the safest way to do that was for me to lie flat on a backboard. They worked in teams, passing me from one to the next over the ductwork. Once that was accomplished, they continued down the open attic staircase and proceeded down the curved staircase leading to the first floor.

Once I was in the ambulance, I asked Bob if he would take care of Halo before going to the hospital. When Bob arrived, an orthopedic surgeon was attending to my ankle, which was broken in three places. Surgery was scheduled for the next morning. Other than keeping me comfortable, there was nothing else to do. I insisted that Bob go back home. I was in good hands.

My surgery went well, but I had to stay in the hospital for several days. I was also informed that I would be in a wheelchair for about three months. Getting me inside our house would not be easy since all the exterior doors had at least two steps. Bob spotted the dog ramp we had used to help Halo following his ligament surgery in our garage and decided to buy another one like it to use for pushing my wheelchair into the house. I was terrified when Bob tried to do just that. The ramps were too short and steep. I was certain the chair would roll back on Bob or that I would topple over the side of it as he struggled to move it forward. Somehow, we made it safely inside.

But once we were inside, we realized that I would not be able to come and go as needed. We contacted two carpenters who had recently done some work for us. They agreed to build a twelve-foot ramp with railings on our back porch. My physical therapist showed me how to go up and down the ramp without assistance. For me, that meant independence. I was able to go up and down. Halo always stayed by my side and was a great assistant, never rushing me or trying to pull on his leash. Dogs always seem to know how to act when things truly matter.

Once I was out of the wheelchair, we decided to donate the ramp to anyone who needed it. One of our friends from church had cancer and could no longer walk. A group of guys from church retrofitted the ramp for her back porch. After she passed away, the ramp was again retrofitted for another person in need. The "wandering ramp" was passed on to one more person that I know of. I like to think that it is still out there helping others.

Sometime in 2012, Bob and I realized that while my mother was still able to take care of herself, it wouldn't be long before that all changed. I drove to Tyler as often as I could, stopping in Vicksburg, Mississippi, at Anchuca Inn on the way to and from. I loved this place, and I felt very safe staying there.

Bob had decided to retire within the following year. Since my mother was already settled in Tyler, that seemed to be the most likely place for us to move. I had been wanting to go back to Texas for many years. The longest place we had ever lived was in West Chester, Pennsylvania. And while I loved most of the places we had resided, I looked forward to "going home."

It took about a year to build our house in Tyler. I went there once a month to see how things were going. When Bob was able to come with me, we also brought Halo since we could stay at my mother's house. Once, we rented a U-Haul truck so we could store things, such as family antiques, that we didn't want the movers to touch. Halo would lie on the floor between our seats the whole trip.

We finally moved into our new home on January 14, 2014. Most of our time from that day on was spent getting settled. We had moved frequently, leaving behind wonderful places and friends. I was glad that we could look after my mother, and for a while, at least, I had family members who lived nearby.

By summer, something was amiss with Halo. He did not have much energy, and one of his eyes protruded. I decided we should take him to the vet's for a checkup. Some of his blood work results were not normal, and other matters required further investigation. We had to take Halo to Dallas for examination and treatment. Fortunately, we were able to schedule an appointment promptly due to the urgency of his condition.

The next day, Bob and I sat in the waiting room with Halo. We were scared of what might be found after his test results. Halo was thirteen at the time, about two months away from being fourteen. Keiko was sixteen and a half when she passed away. It didn't seem fair that Halo may not live as long as she did.

My heart broke when we heard Halo's diagnosis. He had a type of nasal cancer that could not be cured. That explained why he had sneezed so frequently during the past few weeks. It was decided that the best treatment for Halo was chemotherapy drugs to help stop the further growth of cancer cells in his nasal cavity. Bob and I frowned upon hearing this, but there didn't seem to be a better alternative. We could administer the pills ourselves, but we needed to continue coming to the clinic in Dallas at least once a week.

There were unpleasant side effects, such as nausea, that made taking his medication difficult. But after a few days of chemo, Halo's protruding eye had almost returned to normal. He was his handsome self again, and I began thinking that maybe he was the lucky dog you sometimes hear about—the one that, despite everything going against him, had somehow beaten all odds.

A day or so later, Halo began sneezing blood nonstop. It was early in the morning before the veterinarian's office opened. All we could do was rush him to the animal emergency clinic, which operated after-hours between six pm and seven-thirty am.

I rode in the backseat with Halo, whose nose had continued to bleed. As Bob drove out of our driveway, we were met with construction trucks on both sides of the street where a new house was being built. Some of the vehicles had their doors wide open, creating a roadblock for anyone trying to get past them. Bob had to honk to get their attention, which only annoyed them.

After we got Halo to the clinic and his nose bleed under control, we took him to our vet's for observation, as suggested, for the rest of the day. After we got home, I walked up to the construction site and pleaded with the workers to park only on one side of the street. I was in tears as I told them that our dog had to have emergency care, and every minute of delay was critical. They agreed to my request, but the very next day, they were back to parking wherever they liked. Not only that, but a Middle Eastern man drove down our cul-de-sac and parked his large pickup in the middle of the road. I was outside weeding flower beds. Halo was feeling much better, so I didn't have to stay nearby. I called out to the man and asked him to park next to the curb. My request infuriated him. He ordered me to go back to my home (as though I would). I told him to leave, which made him even angrier. He got in his truck and drove up a bit, then turned around and drove slowly as I walked back to our house. He then blocked my driveway with his vehicle. I went inside and called the police. By the time they arrived, the man was long gone. The police did nothing and didn't seem to take my concerns seriously. Halo would have made better protection had he not been ill.

A couple of days later, Halo seemed to be feeling much better. We were ecstatic, believing that the cancer pills were working. We spent all day playing with him and enjoying sitting next to him. He almost seemed like his old self. I believe in miracles, no matter how rare they may be.

When tomorrow arrived, our hope crumbled. Halo did not feel good at all. Most of the time, he hid under a table or chair. He did not want us to pet him, and he refused any food we offered him. It was so upsetting, but there was little we could do to make him feel better.

It had been a long day, and we hoped he could sleep rather than stay awake all night. The evening faded, so Bob took Halo outside, hoping he was ready for bed. I watched from inside the kitchen. Twice, Halo buckled his knees into the grass, signaling he was too weak to walk any further. Bob helped him up and guided him into the kitchen.

Halo slowly walked over to his water bowl and drank a small amount of water. He then walked toward me, where I was standing next to the sink. When he reached me, he folded his front legs beneath him and gently lay on the floor. I saw the light leave his eyes and felt the stillness of his breath and heard the silence of his heart that no longer beat.

The magnitude of my grief cannot be described. It was uncanny how much Halo's illness and passing mimicked my brother's final days. Both of them had died of blood cancer, and both had passed away just three weeks after being diagnosed. Both were around the same age, fourteen, and both will remain in my heart forever.

Halo left us on a hot, steamy evening in August. We didn't know what to do, so we contacted the animal emergency clinic. They gave us instructions for keeping Halo's body until we could take him to the vet's for cremation. We decided to place him in Keiko's Radio Flyer wagon, which we had kept in the garage for all these years. Halo had never wanted to use it and jumped out of it if we tried to give him a ride. Once we had him in the wagon, we wrapped him in a blanket and surrounded him with several bags of ice to prevent him from decomposing. The biggest heartbreak was surrendering him to the veterinarian to be transformed into ashes, so we could put them in a keepsafe box like we did with Keiko. A dog's life is much too short, but perhaps God meant it that way to teach us how to live.

"Unlike humans, dogs don't wrestle with who they are. They come into this world knowing how to live.
If they have a problem,
it's most likely that we are the cause."
— *Patricia Taylor Wells*

KASPAR'S STORY

October 21, 2014

WE WAITED SIX weeks after Halo passed, just like we did with Keiko, to search for another dog. We wanted to ensure, of course, that the breeder we chose did not have hidden issues, like Steve in Pennsylvania had. I found a breeder about a hundred and fifty miles from us, north of Denton, Texas. The owner, Snopuf American Eskimos, had several Eskies displayed online that were currently available for adoption. I kept going back to one in particular who was not only as cute as a button, but seemed to have a mind of his own. We agreed to meet the breeder at a shopping mall halfway between their location and ours. We were excited about having a dog again. The only thing we didn't like was his American Kennel Club registration name, "Bend it Like Beckham." His call name was "Beckham," but even that did not suit us. Perhaps the breeder had a reason for the name, but we decided to go with something else.

After reviewing numerous names in a baby name book, we found the one we favored: Kaspar. We used the German spelling to avoid anyone associating him with "Casper the Friendly Ghost." According to German roots, the name means "treasurer," but I am more inclined to think of it as the "treasure" Kaspar has become over the years.

One of the Three Wise Men, or Magi, who is believed to have presented gifts to Baby Jesus, was also named Kaspar. Whether or not the name begins with "C" or "K" or if the ending is "ar" or "er" is a matter of preference.

Kaspar was born on October 21, 2014, about two months after Halo passed away. It was mid-January when we adopted him at three months old. He was a bit smaller than Halo, but just as handsome. It wasn't easy to know what to expect of Kaspar since Halo was ten months old when we got him. By then, he was no longer a baby, like Kaspar, when he came to live with us.

When we pulled up at the parking lot of the shopping mall, we heard a dog barking, but did not see it. After we exited our car, we walked over to the Rocky Mountain Chocolate Factory, where we were to meet our new puppy. Beckham, as he was called then, put up quite a resistance when he saw us. He had a high-pitched voice that I'm sure everyone at the mall could hear. We had brought along a cage for the ride back home, but he wanted nothing to do with it. I picked him up so I could hold him in my lap.

Kaspar continued to squeal, and I could barely keep him from crawling up on my shoulder as he tried to break away from me. Bob was having a difficult time driving, so he pulled over so I could get in the back seat with our hysterical puppy. I was beginning to think that we had made a bad choice.

Once we were home, Kaspar settled down. He was still unsure of us, but that was to be expected. He didn't know yet just how much we would love him, no matter how difficult he might be.

We decided to let Kaspar sleep on our bed that night. I had bought him a floppy, long plush toy with a dog's face and a squeaker that he could bite down on. Keeping him on the bed was not that easy. I had never seen a dog as squirmy as he was. He could jump off the bed, but couldn't get back on it without help. He whined a lot, too.

First nights, though, never go well. All we could do was be patient and hope for the best. When I was growing up, I remember that my parents always put a new puppy in a cardboard box lined with a small blanket or towel. To top it off, my father placed a ticking clock under the cover. Supposedly, the sound of the clock would mimic the heartbeat of the puppy's mother. I don't know if that truly worked, or if the puppy just grew tired of the endless ticking and fell asleep.

My mother especially liked Kaspar, and he always showed respect when she was around. Any other strangers were not received very well. In April of 2015, I gave my mother a ninetieth birthday party at our home. That meant that Kaspar had to spend the day at a kennel, since he grabbed any food he could get his hands on, and we weren't sure how he would behave with so many people around. Altogether, thirty-five guests planned to attend the party. It was a happy occasion, and when I look back, I am grateful for having made all the arrangements and basically, doing all the work involved. A number of the people there are no longer with us. People and pets, especially dogs, are what make life special.

But there was also a sadness brewing that I was not yet aware of. One of my best friends from college suffered an aneurysm the same weekend as my mother's birthday party. I did not know this until late September. Although my friend had survived the aneurysm, she was unable to speak, walk, or care for herself. She was transferred to a nursing home until she died a few months later. I was devastated, but having Kaspar to hold and love was a huge help.

One early morning in July, Bob took Kaspar outside. We were the first house built on our street, followed by two other homes that were still under construction at the time. All the other lots were wooded. Suddenly, Kaspar pulled on his leash and gave a shrill bark. Bob turned to where Kaspar had his eyes fixed. Twenty-five feral hogs were standing on the curb, one lot away from us. One of them weighed at least five hundred pounds. Bob quickly scooped Kaspar up and ran inside. I thought Bob was joking when he told me about the hogs. I looked out the window as they crossed the street and disappeared into the woods.

Texas has the highest number of feral hogs in the United States. These nocturnal creatures are known for destroying lawns, parks, and golf courses. They can be very dangerous, especially if cornered or wounded. Our security cameras captured the hogs tearing up my flower beds one night. I posted the video on YouTube and paired it with Johann Strauss II's *The Blue Danube*. We hired a licensed hunter to trap them, but that didn't completely resolve the problem. I heard the pigs a few nights later outside our backyard fence and decided to get rid of them in another way. I scared them off by blowing on a safety signal horn. It was so loud that it woke up a couple of neighbors across the lake from us. The hogs never came back after that.

We also faced other dangers in our neighborhood. Bob and I had become aware that drug dealers were using the wooded lots on our street for peddling illegal substances. The street we lived on ended in a cul-de-sac. We were the only house, other than three others, that were closer to the entrance. The deals were usually made around the same time after dark. The buyers would drive down our street, circle the cul-de-sac, flash their lights, and then park their vehicles. We would see a flash of light coming from the woods a few minutes later. The buyer would get out of their car or truck and disappear into the woods. A short time later, the buyer would get back in their vehicle and leave. We contacted the police, but most of the time, the dealers and buyers were long gone by the time they arrived.

One time, though, two college-age boys drove into the cul-de-sac. But instead of coming full circle, they stopped halfway and flashed their lights. Nothing happened. We knew, of course, that they had not followed instructions, which left the drug dealers uncertain as to who they were. As usual, we called the police. When they got there, the two boys were still waiting in their car. But since they had not purchased any drugs, the police sent them on their way.

Another time, Kaspar alerted us after hearing voices in the dark. We looked out the window to see what was going on. A pickup truck was parked next to our driveway, and five guys were walking around in the cul-de-sac. Our neighbor across from us was coming home when he saw four of the guys jump in the bed of the truck. The driver stepped on the gas as the others lay down in the back to avoid detection. Our neighbor didn't even bother to turn around. Instead, he backed out of our street, then chased the pickup till they were several streets over and out of sight.

Not long after that event, the police installed a large security camera on a tree visible to anyone entering the cul-de-sac. Between the camera and more new houses being built on our street, the drug dealing came to an end.

Kaspar was always intrigued when something unusual was happening. He was right there with us every time we looked out the window. Dogs can sense fear and are keen observers of posture, movement, and other signals, such as changes in voice or behavior.

Of all the things there were to fear, fireworks were number one on Kaspar's list, followed by thunder. Either one caused him to go berserk. We dreaded the Fourth of July and New Year's Eve. We tried wrapping

"I'm suspicious of people who don't like dogs, but I trust a dog when it doesn't like a person."
— *Bill Murray*

him in a ThunderShirt, giving him medication to settle his nerves, and turning on multiple fans in our bedroom to block sound. Often, the fireworks lasted two to three hours after midnight. And even though they were against the law in city limits, no one ever stopped them. The noise was frustrating, not only for humans and pets, but also for wildlife of every kind.

In November, we traveled to Lacey, Washington, where Bob's father, Lee, lived. It was his ninety-seventh birthday, and aside from vision issues, he was in pretty good health. Although the independent living place where he lived also offered assisted living, he refused to go there. Instead, he hired people to take care of him twenty-four hours a day in his home.

We had to leave Kaspar at the kennel for several days while we were away, which he did not like one bit. We had previously enrolled him in the Puppy Education, Intermediate Education, and Advanced Learning Training Program, sponsored by PetSmart. While Kaspar was smart enough to pass the training requirements, he also knew how to break the rules.

Eskies are known for their agility. It was the circus that made them popular. The first dog to ever walk a tightrope was an American Eskimo Dog named Pierre, who performed with the

Barnum and Bailey Circus in the 1930s. We soon discovered that Kaspar could walk on his hind legs, both forward and backward. He usually did this to scope out unknown humans or dogs, or anything else that seemed out of place to him. The workers building the house across the street from us stopped what they were doing and gathered around Kaspar to watch him walk on his hind legs, somewhat like a hula dancer, as he swayed his front legs side to side in the air.

Between the last half of 2015 and the first half of 2016, we established more connections with members of the Tyler community. I also enjoyed having family nearby, something I had missed over the years, once we moved from Houston to other states throughout the U.S. But even so, I wasn't as fulfilled as I had hoped to be. It wasn't easy to make new friends in Tyler. Our social life was mainly based on attending community or charitable events. After living here for over ten years, it still is.

My life was about to change, though, in ways I had dreamed of but never thought would happen. A friend of ours invited us to tour Camp Tyler, where he worked, after learning that I had attended the Tyler icon in elementary school. I was surprised that no one had written a book about the camp. The camp's director suggested that I write one since I had brought up the idea. I had written things all my life, but never managed to finish or improve anything I had put on paper. Penning this story was my chance, and I took it.

Camp Tyler, A First of Its Kind was published in mid-2016. An anonymous donor covered the printing costs, and I transferred the copyright to the camp. The picture on the front cover is from an article featured in *The Saturday Evening Post* on March 8, 1952. Camp Tyler was one of the outdoor education schools included in the magazine.

I received many benefits from writing this book. I was interviewed on a local television station and was mentioned in several news articles. Bob and I were featured in *Tyler Neighbors South* magazine. We were even on the front cover along with Kaspar.

A great deal happened in 2016. My mother was beginning to have problems, not only with her health but with daily tasks. Her air conditioning went out in July and was not repaired until two weeks later. During this time, Mother's chihuahua, Hannah, passed away. It was very sad, and there was no way to make her loss less painful. Bob and I were also impacted by the stress of caring for Mother and trying to decide what we needed to do to make her life easier.

I had also begun working on a manuscript that I had spent several years writing, but I was never able to let it go. While attending a writer's conference, I had an opportunity to meet with one of the speakers about not wanting to publish my unfinished novel because I was afraid of what my family would think. He quickly replied that anyone who thought that way shouldn't be a writer. That motivated me to write the story in multiple points of view, which allowed me to express not only my side of the story but also the perspectives of all those involved. Within a few weeks after sending a query, I had a publisher. I am pleased to say that Bedazzled Ink Publishing remains my publisher.

Even so, Bob and I were overwhelmed with everything going on in our lives. Part of our stress was related to Kaspar, who could be challenging at times. We decided to place Kaspar in a special training program for an entire month. We inspected Circle Star Pet Resort, located approximately forty miles away, and found it to be very desirable. We were anxious, though, about not seeing him for so long. Would he even remember us?

On August 1, we dropped Kaspar off at Circle Star and departed for a road trip to the Finger Lakes. The beautiful scenery helped us unwind and not fret over being away from Kaspar. We were able to see several friends and family members from places we had previously lived. I felt a bit of melancholy throughout our trip and wondered if we had been better off staying put. At the same time, I felt grateful for having lived in various places.

Once we were back in Texas, all we could think of was seeing Kaspar again. We had missed him so much. But when we picked him up at Circle Star, he didn't seem to have missed us at all. I worried that he was confused and perhaps thought we had abandoned him. Within a day or two, though, all was well.

Whenever we had to drive Kaspar somewhere, he insisted on sitting in the front seat. That meant that I had to ride in the back. Kaspar also sat backward so he could look at me. Although he had a seatbelt to keep him safe, I never felt entirely sure about it.

I had also delved into social media, which I had always claimed I would never take part in. But now that I had published the Camp Tyler book and my novel, *The Eyes of the Doe*, would be published in 2017, I realized the benefit of having it to promote my work. Another advantage was that I could snap photos of Kaspar and share what a beautiful boy he was.

Sadly, Bob's father passed away late in September. He was ninety-eight years old. I dreaded having to board Kaspar again so we could attend his funeral in Washington state. At least Kaspar seemed to tolerate being at Circle Star. The dogs there were kept very busy with various activities throughout the day. Best of all, the camp staff members took photos of each dog staying at the camp and posted them on Facebook. It helped assure us that he was doing well.

In the meantime, my mother required increasing assistance. We tried using an at-home senior living service, but that didn't work out very well. My niece, a nurse, was assisting Mother with her medications, but there were issues with that, also. Mother did not want to move to an assisted living facility. We could certainly understand that, but we also knew we were headed in that direction.

Kaspar had his share of trouble, too. He had a bad habit of sneaking things into his mouth, then hiding them in his cheeks. He usually chose between bark mulch or prickly sweet gum balls that fell to the ground every autumn. He even stashed the balls into both cheeks before we realized what he was doing. There were a few times when we had to rush him to the animal emergency for X-rays to determine what he had swallowed. Most of the time, we were able to stick our fingers into his mouth and retrieve what he was hiding. We eventually decided that the safest thing to do was to keep Kaspar on a leash even in our fenced backyard. He still tries to eat things, including the frequent hair he sheds, but we've managed to keep better track of him.

Since we've had Kaspar, I've called him a variety of nicknames, including Buddy, Baby, Mister, Pumpkin, Puppy Boy, and Little Samolian. Since the latter is not particularly common, I looked into its origins. My father always called my brother and me "Little Samolian," but we never knew what it meant or signified. Interestingly, the name is often used when referring to the Samoyed dog breed. These dogs are frequently mistaken for American Eskimo Dogs. Samoyeds are larger than Eskies, but both have beautiful, fluffy white coats and tails that curl over their backs. Both breeds are members of the spitz family and are considered sweet, friendly, and cute.

"My fashion philosophy is, if you're not covered in dog hair, your life is empty."
— Elayne Boosler

In the Fall, I began yoga lessons. I had tried to teach myself, but with little success. A friend of mine was a yoga instructor, so I decided to take private lessons from her. I was amazed at what my body could do by learning the correct poses and movements, along with continued practice.

Dogs naturally engage in stretching and movements that are somewhat similar to yoga, such as the downward dog and play bow poses. There is even a yoga practice known as "doga," which combines dogs and their owners participating together in stretching sessions.

We finally arranged for Mother to move to an assisted living facility at the beginning of February 2017. When we came over to her house a couple of days before her move, we found her on the floor. We had to call 911 to take her to the hospital. Fortunately, she did not have any broken bones, but she had to spend about three weeks in rehab before she could be admitted to her new care facility.

While looking forward to the release of *The Eyes of the Doe* on November 1, I began writing another book based on my time spent in Paris, France, studying at the Sorbonne during the summer of 1968. The political unrest in May had nearly brought down the French government. I was caught in the middle of a student/worker riot that occurred on Bastille Day. The title of my book, *Mademoiselle Renoir à Paris*, was based on the nickname one of my French professors had given me.

I traveled to Paris in October 2017 with two friends. It was interesting to see how much the City of Lights had changed. I found the dorm where I had lived and other familiar places I had visited many years before. Bob and I had decided not to let Mother know I was out of the country until I was back home.

Aside from the Camp Tyler book, I had not mentioned anything to Mother or some of my other family members about my novel or the memoir I was currently working on. I felt that *The Eyes of the Doe* was too sensitive, since the story was wrapped around the sudden loss of my brother due to cancer. And while the current memoir would not have that effect, it would most likely lead a trail back to the novel.

This type of circumstances would not occur in the dog world. In general, dogs live in the moment, relying more on instinct while reacting to their current surroundings and immediate needs. They don't plan for the future or worry about things that may never happen. Dogs are capable of associating sights and sounds with routines, events, and patterns. Kaspar, for example, gets excited when he hears utensils rattle or his food being prepared. He knows it's dinnertime and barks until his bowl is filled.

> *"Dogs are not our whole life, but they make our lives whole."*
> — *Roger Caras*

I was beginning to realize that there were several differences between Kaspar and our other Eskies. Kaspar had only lived in one home, whereas Keiko and Halo had moved not only to several houses but also to locations throughout the United States. However, Bob and I had traveled more often and for more extended periods, which meant he was boarded more often than they were. Kaspar also seemed to understand what we were saying and what it meant to a higher degree. He was also more stubborn and enjoyed playing runaway games, knowing he was too fast for us to catch him. Even so, we loved him, no matter what he did.

At some point, Kaspar began getting up in the middle of the night and going to a corner. He scratched the floor and didn't stop. One of us had to get out of bed and go over to where he was. Strangely, he seemed to be in a trance, as though he was sleepwalking. According to some, Kaspar may be following instinctual behavior or a dog's natural tendency to prepare a sleeping area, or a sign of stress or medical issues.

In late December, I began practicing aerial yoga. I had changed instructors and studios, and I felt more confident in my performance. It fascinated me to watch yoga enthusiasts hang from the ceiling by silk scarves. At the same time, it also left me anxious to think that I could support my body with such flimsy means. I was surprised once I tried it, how easy it was to perform aerial poses. My favorite position was hanging upside down with my hands folded together like a prayer. Later, my cousin Brenda joined me for several sessions, which were enjoyable for both of us.

The owner of the studio kept several rescued kittens in a back room. She was devoted to finding permanent homes for abandoned or lost felines. I had never been around cats, and was a bit nervous if they came too close to me. Gradually, I became very fond of them and loved it when they snuggled up next to me as I lay on my back, especially during Shavasana, the final pose of a yoga session. Often, one of my favorite kitties lay on top of me as I practiced deep relaxation.

I wondered what Kaspar thought of this. I'm sure he could detect the scent of the cats when I came home from the studio. He never fussed about it, however. I had always believed that dogs hated cats, but apparently, that is not the case. Some dogs enjoy chasing cats, but mostly they are being playful rather than aggressive. I even found that being around the kittens

"Dogs only want love, but cats demand worship."
— Lucy Maud Montgomery

was somewhat more calming than being around dogs. I wouldn't say that to Kaspar, though.

"My idea of absolute happiness is to be in bed on a rainy day with my blanket, my cat and my dog."
— *Anne Lamott*

Overall, 2018 was a time to settle and enjoy what we could when we could. Mother had accepted that the assisted living facility was now her home. Her life had changed in a way no one wants it to, yet many of her worries had disappeared. Bob and I took turns visiting her almost every day. We did that to avoid wearing ourselves out. On weekends, we came together to see her. Whenever possible, we brought her over to our house for lunch or an early dinner. She lit up the moment she saw Kaspar, and I do not doubt that he felt the same toward her.

My writing had taken off in many ways. I was finishing up *Madamoiselle Renoir à Paris*, and had hired an artist I knew to illustrate scenes from 1968 newspapers and magazines. My novel, *The Eyes of the Doe*, won first prize for family life fiction in the Best of Texas Book Awards sponsored by Texas Authors. But the most remarkable thing of all was that I was finally writing the poetry that had drawn me to it most of my life. I woke every morning and looked all around. Eventually, inspiration came, and I found it difficult to do anything else for the rest of the day.

I was also asked to speak to various groups and organizations. Public speaking was not something that came easily for me. I don't think I ever raised my hand in the classroom. However, my life has undergone significant changes over the past few years, and I am grateful for them.

By now, Kaspar was three years old. He loved playing with his Frisbee. He caught it in the air, ran off with it, and finally brought it back to us, though most of the time he wouldn't let go of it. Since his Frisbee had a hole in the middle, he either clinched it with his teeth for a tug of war or stick his nose through the hole, covering his eyes, then running off again. He always looked so funny. We even bought him two Frisbees with a hole that he could play with indoors, which comes in handy when the weather is too hot or cold, or it's raining.

But even though things had settled down for the time, we knew that darkness was rushing toward us. Mother had begun to wander outside of the community where she lived, and she often believed that she was having conversations with my deceased father and others. The staff found it challenging to keep her safe, and they suggested that before long, she would have to move to a memory care facility. The assisted living director did not hide the fact that we should find a better place for her to live. I don't think I've ever felt so helpless. Each evening, I cuddled up with Kaspar, lying there while he soaked up all my anxiety.

It was near the end of July when we decided to move Mother to a different place with more options for her care. She was only at the new place for one week when we were told that she had to move to memory care. Fortunately, the rooms for both assisted living and memory care were identical in size and accommodation. The main difference between the units was the permanently locked exit door, which prevented memory care residents from leaving without assistance.

> *"Dogs are a reminder that even in our darkest moments, there is always love and joy to be found."*
> — *Kendle Frank*

It was sad to see my mother's life so limited. She had always been a hard worker and had remained independent up to this point. But now, every day, I saw her life slipping away. It was ironic, though, that despite her memory loss, she occasionally talked about people and things from long ago. Some of her tales were new to me, and I treasured every moment she spoke of them.

By the time the year had ended, I had finished writing my first collection of poetry and submitted it for publication. *LodeStar* was my most prized work. My whole life was spread throughout its pages. Composing it was both painful and magnificent. Yet, somehow, wading through reflections of light and dark helped make me whole. This, and having Kaspar by my side.

*"Dogs come into our lives
to teach us about love.
They depart to teach us
about loss.
A new dog never replaces
an old dog; it merely
expands the heart."*
— *Erica Jong*

I had realized that you cannot pile new grief on top of old grief, hoping to bury it. There is no limit to how much misery life may throw at us, or any guarantee of how much of it we can withstand. I tried to focus on what little time we still had, but every time the clock chimed, I felt the loss of each hour rushing past me. Our minister came to see Mother one day. He pulled out his cell phone and raised the volume so Mother could hear the sweet strain of gospel music. Within seconds, she was singing every word by heart, and in every word there was a meaning that had carried her through every sorrow she had known.

During this time, Mother was transferred to hospice care. I found it interesting how the hospice care team could calculate how much longer my mother might live. I wondered if the same goes for dogs or other animals. Are there signs that tell them what to expect and how to deal with it?

I kept busy taking care of everything needed for the publication of my book. The release date for *LodeStar* was April 12, 2019. I wondered if maybe I should postpone it for now. The hospice team had narrowed the time they felt before Mother passed. I didn't want to hear their opinion.

I stayed home all morning on Friday, April 12. Bob and I decided to wait until noon to visit Mother. Even though I was excited about the release of my book, I felt guilty about sending out release notices to friends and acquaintances on social media. I also disliked not feeling comfortable enough to share my writing with Mother and other family members.

Later that day, when we walked through the doors of the hospice facility, one of the nurses came up to us. She gently told us that Mother would most likely pass sometime this evening. I wanted to scream at her. How did she know this?

When Bob and I entered Mother's room, she was sleeping. We stayed with her all afternoon. I finally persuaded Bob to go back home to feed Kaspar and take care of him for a while. Fortunately, it was only a five-minute drive from our home to the care center. Mother continued to sleep without ever waking up. I had not anticipated that I might not ever get to speak to her again. When Bob returned, I went home for a short time.

By the time I came back, the evening sky was waning. Mother was still sleeping. Her breathing had become more irregular, alternating between shallow and deep gasps of air. It was agonizing to watch her, especially knowing that there was nothing we could do to help her escape what eventually becomes everyone's fate. I placed a chair next to Mother's bed so I could be close to her and hold her hand. I will never forget that what I felt instead was her holding my hand. I realized that she was struggling to help me let go of her. As difficult as it was, I understood now that that was what she wanted.

I stood up and kissed Mother's forehead as I let go of her hand. Bob and I told the hospice staff to call us if anything changed. As soon as we arrived home, the phone rang. Mother had passed during our short drive. We quickly attended to Kaspar's needs and then drove back to the care center.

When we walked into her room, Mother's right arm was raised in the air, as though she was caught between life and death while reaching for heaven. Later, I learned this type of spasm is widespread at the moment of death. It is eerie, though, and seems somewhat mystical.

The hospice nurse was required to stay with Mother's body until someone from the funeral home, which was down the street, arrived and took over. Bob and I were exhausted, so we went back home since there was nothing else for us to do. Kaspar was anxious but glad to see us. I called my sister, who lived in Waco, and a couple of other people. Everything else would have to wait until the next day.

We buried Mother a few days later at a family plot in East Texas that had belonged initially to my paternal grandparents. It was here that my father and my brother were also buried. The loss of my mother marked a new phase in my life. The fact that Mother had passed the same day, April 12, as the release of my first poetry collection was symbolic for me. The comfort she could never give me following my brother's death no longer mattered. Mother was now replaced by everything I wrote.

Most of my time over the next few months was spent finalizing my mother's estate. It isn't easy to rummage through someone's personal belongings and then decide what to do with them. I even discovered some things I never knew about my mother. Sometimes Kaspar joined me as I sorted through boxes. It was comforting to have him nearby.

I attended aerial yoga sessions more frequently, hoping to escape the sadness that kept me awake each night and filled me with dread each morning. I had very little family left, and the few remaining family members rarely paid any attention to Bob or me. Without Kaspar, I doubt I could have carried on. At least not very well.

> *"Dogs always know when to rest their chin on someone's knee."*
> — *Patricia Taylor Wells*

We decided to spend a few days in Dallas, even though we hated having to board Kaspar. We visited the Botanical Gardens, the JFK Museum, the George W. Bush Presidential Library and Museum, and the Holocaust Museum. Getting away helped somewhat, though later we viewed our trip as a crossing between one loss and another.

Once we were back home, I was eager to resume my yoga practice. I felt invigorated after hanging upside down, swinging back and forth, with one arm almost sweeping the floor while the other clutched the silk yoga scarf that held me aloft. My instructor and I sat together afterward, primarily discussing my progress while one of the studio kittens cuddled up in my lap. I heard a strange, mechanical-like noise, but quickly decided it was coming from one of the trucks at the nearby repair shop.

I went home for a few minutes, then decided to go to the grocery store. My cellphone rang as I walked down the vegetable aisle. My cousin Steve was on the line, but I could barely hear him. It sounded like multiple people were on the line, as though I was picking up conversations of other shoppers. Once back home, I put away the groceries and began to prepare dinner. I suddenly stopped in the middle of what I was doing and told Bob that something was very wrong. He had no idea what I was talking about. I told him I didn't feel well, and he had to finish making dinner. By the time I walked into our bedroom, I was extremely nauseated. It felt like my forehead was on fire from dripping sweat that ran down to my shoulder blades. I began to throw up profusely, and my whole body shook with weakness. I called out for Bob as I made my way to our bed. Kaspar got there first and barked, sounding an alarm for Bob to hurry.

As bad as things were, they were about to get even worse. Suddenly, my head was spinning, and the walls seemed to be coming at me in all directions. I could barely walk, but somehow managed to throw myself on the bed. Once I was lying down, I felt slightly better, but as soon as I raised my head, a hefty dose of vertigo took over. Bob decided to call 911. He put Kaspar in another room while waiting for the ambulance. When the paramedics arrived, they checked my vital signs and asked me numerous questions about how I felt. They quickly determined that I should be transferred to the hospital. As soon as I arrived, several tests were performed. Although there was no indication of anything significant, I was admitted to the hospital.

Once I was settled, I picked up the phone to order something to drink. The line was dead. My nurse, however, was able to make the call for me. I assumed that I had not dialed the phone properly. The very next morning, the same thing happened. The phone wouldn't work for me without having someone's help.

Around seven am, a nurse practitioner, along with a physical therapist, entered my room, demanding that I get out of bed and begin vestibular rehabilitation exercises. I was still experiencing vertigo and was too weak to stand up. The nurse got right in my face and admonished me for performing aerial yoga at my age. She was the meanest healthcare worker I had ever encountered. Her next move was to announce that I was being discharged from the hospital. But her final blow was yet to come.

I tried calling Bob, but once again, I couldn't get the phone to work. Once Bob finally made it to the hospital, we left as soon as I was cleared to go.

There was a strong thunderstorm once we were back home. After it had stopped raining, I decided to return a missed call from the day before. Now, it seemed, our home phone was out of order, most likely from the storm. Bob picked up the receiver, and with a serious look on his face, he told me that there was nothing wrong with the phone. That's when I first learned that I had lost all hearing in my left ear.

Since it was Sunday, I had to wait until Monday to contact my doctor for a referral. I became frantic when I learned that my primary doctor was out of the country. I had also contacted the hospital, only to discover that my discharge papers were useless for obtaining the referral I needed for an ENT (ear, nose, and throat doctor) since the nurse practitioner did not provide relevant information about my condition. My hearing was never checked despite my complaints about the phone service.

On Tuesday, I made an appointment with a family practice doctor who was able to refer me to an ENT. However, the appointment wasn't available until eleven days later. Everything was going against me. Kaspar knew something was wrong and stayed close to me. Time was running out, according to the research I had done regarding my hearing loss.

Several tests were performed during my appointment with the ENT. I was diagnosed with Sudden Sensorineural Hearing Loss (SSHL) in my left ear. The standard treatment for this condition was the use of oral steroids and antibiotics to reduce inflammation. Later, steroids were injected directly through my eardrum. The longer the treatment is delayed, however, the more likely the results will fail. I blamed the nurse practitioner for this. She had ignored symptoms and was more focused on my lifestyle than on my medical condition. Several critical days passed without treatment because of her hasty decision to discharge me from the hospital before determining why I had ended up in the emergency room in the first place.

I spent the next three months undergoing therapy to improve my balance, difficulty in understanding speech, and dealing with the emotional and social impact that the loss of hearing had created. The most important thing I did, however, was to accept what had happened and to let go of it.

I decided it was a good time to start working on a novel I had tried to write many years ago. Thus far, I had written only one chapter based on the time I spent in Saudi Arabia in the 1980s. One of the things holding me back was the amount of research I would have to do to tell a credible story. It wasn't long before I was off and running. Even so, it took me almost two years to complete my cherished novel, *The Sand Rose*.

In early November, we took a road trip across the Northeast. We stopped in various places where we had previously lived so we could visit with former neighbors and friends. Once we arrived in Pennsylvania, we took a train to New York City. We had dinner one evening with three of Bob's cousins and their spouses. Bob's nephew was also in New York at the same time, so we got to visit with him, too. Most of the time, he lived in Athens, Greece. We thoroughly enjoyed the trip. It was especially beneficial for me, having lost both my mother and my hearing in one ear. As always, I hated having to board Kaspar for such a long time. But once he was back home with us, all was well.

But the year wasn't over, and there was something more waiting for us. In late December, Bob had developed a severe cough and fever that wasn't responding to the over-the-counter nonprescription drugs he had taken. I took him to the emergency room, but the tests performed did not reveal the usual flu or viral infection. While no one denied that Bob was ill, they could not identify what had caused his ailment.

Bob speculated that his illness was transmitted by a couple who had just returned from a foreign country, who sat at our table at a Christmas party. This same couple was thought to have attended an earlier gathering, after which they and several others fell ill to an unknown infection.

It was March 2020 before the World Health Organization (WHO) declared this mysterious new illness that originated in Wuhan, China, and was referred to as COVID-19, a pandemic. Very soon, the world shut down. People were scared, and there were many deaths caused by the disease, especially among the older population. Schools, churches, businesses, employers, social activities, restaurants, and just about anything involving close contact with others were either canceled or restricted. Social distancing became the norm, and wearing masks was mandatory.

We continued eating out at our favorite pizza place on Fridays. It gave us a sense of freedom to do so. The events of one Friday in December, however, ended that tradition. We had left the restaurant and were stopped four cars behind a traffic light. I heard a sudden bang and felt our vehicle being pushed into the one ahead of us, which, in turn, hit the car ahead of them. Bob got out of our Toyota 4-Runner to determine what had happened. The driver of the Land Cruiser behind us was attempting to recharge his cellphone when he ran into us at full speed. Fortunately, no one was hurt. The car in front of us had two young children in the backseat of a small sedan. Had the Land Cruiser struck them instead of us, there could have been injuries.

Our Toyota should have been totaled, but our insurance company insisted on repairing it, despite the frame being damaged. The repairs took over one hundred days. Based on what we were told by several car dealers, replacing the frame would not necessarily guarantee that the damages were fully taken care of. We decided to sell the Toyota, but none of the dealers in Tyler wanted a vehicle with this kind of history. We were also told that we probably wouldn't get a fair price because of this. We took the car to CarMax, and to our surprise, we sold it for much more than we had expected.

I always try to find something positive when bad things occur. I was grateful that Kaspar had not been in the Toyota when we were hit. Since Kaspar rides in the front seat with his face turned backward towards me, he could have been injured by the force of the crash. I still feel uneasy when we take Kaspar anywhere, even though he wears a dog seat safety belt to keep him restrained.

The week after our wreck, the pizza place shut down. We still talk about it. We always looked forward to going there. With all that was going on due to the pandemic, it was a welcome retreat, somewhat like a safe harbor, that kept us sane.

It was 2021 before a COVID-19 vaccine was available. However, it was met with much opposition. By then, lockdowns were taking their toll on mental health. It wasn't just humans that were stressed by our new way of life, but also our pets, who often picked up the negative vibes we were sending to them and the world. The most difficult loss for many of us was the loss of friends and family members who disagreed with our views regarding the pandemic, vaccine, and other treatments available. Sadly, most of these relationships have never been revived.

Record-breaking amounts of snow fell in February, initially offering a welcome event from the lockdowns. Kaspar was in awe and spent much of his time perched on an armchair so he could see the fantasy world being created right before his eyes. We were amazed at how quickly the birds had stripped our six holly trees of their berries. Everything froze over the ten days of the storm, commonly called "Snowmageddon." There were widespread power outages, and it wasn't safe to drive anywhere. We had stocked up on supplies early on, but mostly, we survived by placing all frozen food in Styrofoam containers and leaving them outside, or by keeping disposable foods like milk in the garage to keep them cold. Fortunately, we had a gas cook stove for cooking and heating water. We slept under multiple quilts and wore layers of clothing to stay warm. Eventually, the snow and ice came to an end, and our daily lives returned to the new normal dictated by the pandemic.

My novel *The Sand Rose* was published and released in May 2021. I immediately began working on my next book, my second poetry collection. Keeping my mind on my work helped me forget what a miserable world we were living in.

Bob's brother Lee III and his wife Alicia visited us in Tyler, Texas, from Idaho in May. We knew this might be the last time we saw Lee, who was battling a medical condition that soon took his life. But we didn't dwell on that. We were just happy having Lee and Alicia in our home. And fortunately, Kaspar was well-behaved most of the time they were here.

Surprisingly, we did venture out on several trips during the pandemic. In August, we spent a few days in Dallas to visit the Immersive Van Gogh Exhibit, which featured 360-degree projections of the painter's artwork. The only drawback was having to wear a mask, especially in the Texas heat.

Later, in December, we took a road trip to Savannah, Georgia, and then to Charleston, South Carolina. We were also able to visit with our friends Janis and Paul as we traveled across Georgia. I wish they could have met Kaspar, especially since they had often taken care of both Keiko and Halo when we lived in Atlanta.

In early January 2022, Bob tested positive for COVID-19. Two days later, I also came down with the disease. So here we were, both feeling lousy while trying to take care of Kaspar, who I'm sure knew we weren't at our best, but wanted his morning and evening meets on time just the same. And where were his morning walks? For the next ten days, nothing was routine. I slept in the guest room most of the time since Bob had a bad cough that kept me awake. My disappearance every night was another puzzle for Kaspar, who preferred to have us all together all of the time.

A couple of weeks after I seemed to have recovered, I began having heart palpitations related to Long Covid. It was several months before all the symptoms went away, and I was declared free of any issues caused by the virus.

Sometime in 2022, we noticed that Kaspar's skin and hair did not look well. His hair was falling out, but in a different way from its normal shedding. It was thin rather than luxurious, and his skin had dark spots throughout his back and belly. There were also some dark areas on his muzzle. He was not the "Dog Beautiful," his breed was known as. Kaspar lost so much hair that we had to buy him a coat to wear during colder days.

In July, we spent a weekend in Plano, Texas. It's one of our favorite places to get away from everything else going on in our lives. Kaspar was doing better, but it would take another year or so for his hair to get back to normal, or at least close to it.

In September, my poetry collection *Kaleidoscope* was released. As usual, I immediately began working on my next manuscript. *Maple Point* is a historic memoir and involved a great deal of research. Fortunately, since this cottage had belonged to Bob's parents until they sold it in 2005, I had direct access to much of the information I needed.

In November, we went to Vicksburg, Mississippi, along with our friends Bill and Donna. It was fun showing them around our favorite bed and breakfast place, Anchuca. The former owner, Tom, invited us over for cocktails at his home across from the mansion. It felt good to get away now that Kaspar was doing better.

Another year had gone by—this one, not at the top of our list. But things were getting better, and that's all that mattered.

When 2023 rolled around, we didn't have much planned. I decided to invite several friends over for a dinner party. I used to do that

*"My little dog—
a heartbeat at my feet."*
— Edith Wharton

all the time, but now it seemed overwhelming. I hated having to board Kaspar, but he would have disrupted everything. Who knows, though, perhaps watching me run after him as he tried to hide party food in his cheeks may have been entertaining for some of my guests. The party turned out well, but was very exhausting. I probably won't do anything like that again.

April brought much sadness with the passing of my niece Julie, who died from heart issues related to a recent bout of COVID. How unjust it seems to live longer than someone of a younger generation. Julie and I had gone our separate ways during recent years, primarily due to disagreements about my mother's care. Why couldn't we have found a way to make amends, I wondered. My heart was filled with so many years before. Interestingly, while some dogs grieve the loss of their human and canine companions, they don't dwell on past events, trying to figure out who was right and who was wrong. It is always too late to change things after they've happened. But it is never too late to forgive and forget so that we can move on.

"The invisible bond that links the members of a family is sometimes the only sanctuary our heart desires."
— *Patricia Taylor Wells*

In may, we decided to go somewhere not too far away. My cousin Steve lived in McKinney, which was about thirty miles from Dallas. We had never been there, so we enjoyed exploring the city's historical downtown just as much as we enjoyed visiting with Steve. We also got to see my Aunt Reba, Steve's mother, who was a hundred and three at the time. One other interesting place we toured was South Fork Ranch, where episodes of the famed TV series *Dallas* were filmed.

My birthday and our anniversary are two days apart in August. Often, we combine the two when celebrating. This time around, we chose Fort Worth to spend a mini vacation rather than having to board Kaspar for more than a few days. I'm sure he liked this plan much better. It was good for us, too.

In October, my cousin Donna, who lives in Tennessee, came to visit us. I also invited Steve and his girlfriend, Carol, who lived in Tyler, to dinner. The nice thing about having a small gathering is that we didn't have to board Kaspar. He knew our guests, and once he realized that, he behaved very well. Early on, we had observed that he felt more secure if a guest was staying overnight with us. I don't know how he came to this conclusion, but for Kaspar, it made sense.

In early December, we took another short trip, this time in our favorite place of all, Anchuca Mansion in Vicksburg, Mississippi. I always feel like I'm home when we go there. Although we had been there multiple times, we had never gone to the Vicksburg Christmas Parade until then. Not having children or other family members nearby has meant we don't celebrate as much during holidays.

On December 12, Bob's brother Lee III succumbed to Primary Progressive Aphasia, the same disease that the actor Bruce Willis has. The disorder causes language difficulties such as speech, word-finding, and understanding language. It's also associated with memory loss and behavior changes. Lee III had not wanted to have a funeral. His wife, Alicia, decided to wait until summer to have a memorial service near Keuka Lake in upstate New York.

Bob's birthday was December 21, so I put together a pizza party for a small group of friends. It was a difficult time for Bob, and definitely not the best birthday he had ever had. Having lost my brother at a very young age, I'm sometimes guilty of reminding others how fortunate they were to have had someone in their life for such a long time. Saying that can be hurtful, even though it's not intended to be.

At least the beginning of the new year looked promising. My book *Maple Point* was released on January 24, 2024. I am delighted that I was able to preserve so much of Bob's family history. The twenty-two summers I spent at Maple Point will always be one of my favorite memories.

Two days later, my cousin Jay's wife passed away. She had been ill for a long time, but even knowing the outcome of someone's life does not keep us from the pain we will eventually feel. Bob and I went to Sandy's memorial service in mid-February, which was held in Oklahoma City.

On February 11, we had a large hailstorm that damaged our roof. For months, roofs were being replaced throughout Tyler. At least the storm wasn't as scary as the one we had in Knoxville several years ago. However, we scooped up Kaspar and quickly moved him to the half bath with us while we waited out the storm. Although Kaspar is terrified of noises like firecrackers and thunder, he seems to understand that he's safe if we take shelter in either the safe room inside the garage or the half bath in the hall.

Near the end of February, one of my best friends died due to a long-term illness. I had known Gayle since I was in the second grade. She had been one of my bridesmaids, and her daughter Christy was our flower girl. I felt very sad and wondered when it would all end. Kaspar understood how I felt and nuzzled up to me.

Our friends Glenda and Jerry visited us during the Historic Tyler Home Tour for 2024. It had become their tradition over the past few years. This year, however, a Total Solar Eclipse took place on April 8. A special symphony was performed to celebrate the event.

I dreaded the next few months. In mid-April, I had to undergo surgery to remove some abnormal cells. Fortunately, none of them were cancerous, and not much to deal with in terms of healing. Early treatment is always the best remedy.

In June, however, I was scheduled for surgery to remove nine screws and one metal plate that held my ankle together since the time it was broken in three places.

After surgery, I had to wear a large boot on my left foot, but at least I could bear weight. The surgery went well, but I was in a lot of pain for close to three months. The worst part of the process was when the stitches were removed. Initially, Kaspar was curious about why I had to wear the boot, but he got over it and accepted his role as my chief comforter.

Things were much better in August. We decided to drive to the Finger Lakes in New York for a small gathering to honor the life of Lee III. Besides us, Alicia, Bob's nephew Brenton, and his family, and two special friends spent several days on Keuka Lake tracking Lee III's favorite places over the years. The best part of our trip was getting to see Maple Point again. We met the current owner, who graciously showed us the improvements she and her husband had made to the cottage. Bob and I will always feel nostalgic about this iconic place, but knowing it is in such good hands is more than we could ask for.

Although we had a wonderful time in the Finger Lakes, our drive to and from Keuka Lake was a nightmare. We had never experienced anything like it before. We were traumatized by the time we got home and have been reluctant to travel anywhere since then.

It was good, though, to see Kaspar again. We were also grateful that his hair had grown back for the most part, and he looked exceptionally well. For now, some of our plans have changed. We have decided to remain in our home in Tyler for as long as we have Kaspar. Previously, we had thought about moving to Mississippi. I don't know if we've made the right decision, but we can always change our minds again—at least some of the time we can.

My short story collection, *Carousel*, was released in November. Probably no one was as surprised as I was that I would have two new releases

"Life is not always what we want it to be, but it is always what we make it to be."
— *Patricia Taylor Wells*

the same year. I already had an idea for my next book—the one I am writing right now.

On November 30, my Aunt Reba passed away at the age of a hundred and five. We celebrated her life in late December in Center, Texas, where she lived most of her life. Although I was born in Natchez, Mississippi, my parents moved back to Center when I was a year old. When I was seven, we moved to Tyler. Seeing the place I had once lived brought back numerous memories of my grandparents. Bob and I drove past their beautiful old home, which was currently for sale.

We had boarded Kaspar for an overnight stay at the new veterinarian's down the street from us while we attended Aunt Reba's funeral. Since we returned home sooner than expected, we decided to pick Kaspar up rather than have him stay overnight. Before we got him, the power suddenly went off in our area. Just as Bob drove into the parking lot at the vet's, two fire engines pulled up alongside him. All the people inside the building were ordered to exit, but the pets were left inside, which disturbed Bob and other pet owners. Fortunately, the incident was a false alarm.

The power came on shortly, and Kaspar was allowed to return home with Bob.

The only thing we had to worry about for the rest of December was the fireworks on New Year's Eve.

And so, it is already August of 2025. It has been a quiet year for the most part, which makes it the perfect time to finish writing. Kaspar's story does not end here, though. He still has a few more years ahead of him. We can only hope that those years will not just be numbers, but stories of love, health, and happiness.

For Kaspar

I promise to love and care for you for the rest of your life.
And when you are gone, my heart will break.
But I wouldn't have it any other way,
For now, I promise, you will never be alone.

References

American Eskimo Dog Fanciers of Greater Philadelphia

American Eskimo Kennels (1926)

American Kennel Club (1994)

Art Goes to School of Delaware Valley

Atlanta Unity Church

Barnum & Bailey Circus (1930's)

"Blue Danube" by Johann Strauss

Henry Kirke Bush-Brown, Sculptor

Children's Program of Northern Ireland

Circle Star Pet Resort

"Dog Whisperer" with Cesar Millan

HRH "Princess Taphene"

Immersive Van Gogh Exhibit

"No Bad Dogs" by Barbara Woodhouse (1982)

Philadelphia Daily News Magazine

Philadelphia SPCA Newsletter

Puppy Education & Advanced Learning sponsored by PetSmart

Reading Newcomers Club of Reading, PA

Red Cross of Tyler, TX

Saturday Evening Post (1942)

Snopuf American Eskimos

South Fork Ranch ("Dallas" TV Series)

Tyler Neighbors South Magazine (2016)

U.S. Ferderal Aviation Administration (FAA)

White Light's "Stardust Imji"

Wonmanog Kennels, Coatsville, PA

World Health Organization (WHO)

Patricia Taylor Wells published her first book in 2016: *Camp Tyler, A First of its Kind* for the benefit of Camp Tyler, the oldest outdoor education school in the country, which she attended as a child. Since then, Ms. Wells has published the following books: *The Eyes of the Doe* 2017 (novel), *Mademoiselle Renoir à Paris* 2018 (memoir), *LodeStar: Reflections of Light and Dark* 2019 (poetry), *The Sand Rose* 2021 (novel), *Kaleidoscope* 2022 (poetry), *Maple Point* 2024 (memoir), and *Carousel* 2024 (short stories)

Her awards include First Place for Family Life/Inspirational Fiction in the Best of Texas Book Awards in 2018 (*The Eyes of the Doe*), First Place for Poetry in the Best of Texas Book Awards in 2020 (*LodeStar: Reflections of Light and Dark*), First Place for Poetry in the Indie Authors Best Book Award in 2023 (*Kaleidoscope*), First Place for Historic Memoir in the Best of Texas Book Awards in 2025 (*Maple Point*), and First Place for Short Stories in the Best of Texas Book Awards in 2025 (*Carousel*).

Since 2016, *Tyler Today Magazine* has featured Ms. Wells ten times in its "Authors Among Us" column, which she helped inspire to benefit local authors.

Ms. Wells, who holds a BA in English and French, facilitated writing critique groups for the Atlanta Writers Club and Knoxville Writers Group. She especially enjoys writing poetry and draws inspiration from the wide range of experiences she gathered from her travels and living in various places.

www.ingramcontent.com/pod-product-compliance
Lightning Source LLC
Chambersburg PA
CBHW021125130626
46554CB00002B/870